ISBN # 0-9622479-2-8

Published by: Quarter Circle A Enterprises
1159 State Highway 450
Newcastle, WY 82701
©1990 by Rhonda Coy Sedgwick and
Wanda McLaughlin Hughes

Designed and printed by: Grelind Printing Center
Rapid City, South Dakota

Bernice McLaughlin

Prairie Trails of Miz Mac

by
Rhonda Coy Sedgwick

Dedication

I dedicate this book to the loving memory of my little Mother, who was Mother and Father both to me from the time I was two years old.

I never knew my Daddy, but I always knew he loved me because of Mother's love for him and for my brother and me. I named my first son for him, Loris.

Mother was my inspiration as a child. Growing up, she taught me to work and to believe in myself. She was always in control of every situation and I thought there was <u>nothing</u> she couldn't do!

Her creed was, "Hard work never hurt anyone. Believe in God and in yourself, and you can become anything you want to be."

She always said, "I would rather wear out than rust out," and she proved it in her 93 active years.

WANDA MC LAUGHLIN HUGHES

CHAPTERS

Acknowledgments

I wish to thank the many individuals whose assistance and support helped make this book a reality. Wanda Hughes is primarily responsible, and I am grateful to her for allowing me the honor of having a part in it.

From the moment Miz Mac and I met, at the National Cowgirl Hall of Fame in the Spring of 1977, we both knew we were kindred spirits. It seemed we'd known each other forever, and a very strong bond was immediately formed. Knowing her and counting her as my friend has been one of my life's great privileges.

My sincere appreciation goes to Riley and Wanda Hughes, Stanley and Marjorie McLaughlin, Beulah Hittson, Reba Garrison, Loris Hughes, Bill Hughes, Howard Hughes, Bruce King, Virginia Wagner, Hugh Cozart, Don Adams, Nikki A. Sharp, Roy Banta, Lynn and Joan Hunsperger, Doyle Kear, Mr. and Mrs. A. D. Weatherly, W.C. Wheatley and Cluvarie Dodson for so generously sharing their recollections and impressions of Miz Mac.

I'm also indebted to my family, Vi and Francis Sedgwick, for their unwavering support during the long and tedious hours of producing the book. They proofread multiple drafts and helped me endure computer failures and many other frustrations.

My sincerest thanks to all of you!

RHONDA COY SEDGWICK

Foreword

The King family knew and admired Bernice McLaughlin for many years, having had a similar background of homesteading in the Estancia Valley that she had in pioneering in Union County.

She had a true pioneer spirit, managing to persevere through many hardships to accomplish the many things she did in her life.

I enjoyed very much working with her on the Highway 370 project and seeing a bridge named in her honor for all of her devotion and work in that effort.

I also always admired her because of her deep and abiding faith in God, which so much reminded me of my own mother.

BRUCE KING

Introduction

When Bernice Walsh was six or eight years old her grandparents moved a house on their prairie homestead in Alberta, Canada, and her greatest desire was to drive the team. Her grandfather granted permission, but there was another problem.

The door of the house had been removed for moving, and Bernice's grandmother admonished her to guard the opening and keep her pet cats out. Utilizing the capacity for quick thought and decisive action which was to characterize her entire life, Bernice promptly collected her cats and appropriated a length of binder twine from her grandfather's barn. Slipping over the hill she deftly employed the binder twine, staking each cat out by a leg.

Grandmother's assigned task dutifully attended, she returned in time to drive the team. Despite her youth, she successfully negotiated the teamster duties connected with the house-moving.

A neighbor, there to assist with the chore, observed the entire scenario and chuckled, "That girl will make a livin' wherever she goes!"

Little did anyone realize what an amazingly prophetic statement that would prove to be. The tiny teamster was destined to become a true pioneer of two nations, leaving a rare, perhaps even unequaled, legacy of determination, endurance and success.

1 Pioneer Heritage

Richard Walsh (1863-1945) was the son of Richard and Mary (Laycock) Walsh of Middleborough, Yorkshire, in Northern England. He grew up there and as part of his traditional English education he was taught the trade of a butcher.

At the age of 18 Richard embarked for the New World, sailing for the shores of Canada from Bradford, England. He landed along the coast of Nova Scotia, probably in the year 1884 or '85. He first settled at Winnipeg, Manitoba, and later lived around Moosomin, Saskatchewan.

Some time later his parents and a younger brother, Jim, also migrated to Canada from the mother country. Still later, another brother, Will, crossed the ocean and settled around Minneapolis, Minnesota, in the United States.

For some time Richard Walsh worked for the Canadian Pacific Railway, which certain Canadian historians call the "most enduring achievement" of the prominent and politically controversial Sir John Macdonald. D.J. McIntyre, manager of the Canada Central Railroad, received a contract in 1880 (through negotiations in London) to build the C.P.R. over a ten year period, receiving a subsidy of $25,000,000 and alternate sections amounting to 25,000,000 acres of land suitable for settlement. Historians estimate that 40,000 workers participated in this monumental construction effort, with rails locomotives, cars and equipment coming from both the United States and Britain.

While working for the railroad, Walsh also participated in the Riel Rebellion. More than a century later, his daughters recalled hearing him tell of "driving a truck" [probably some kind of small railroad vehicle used for carrying supplies] during the Riel Rebellion.

Sometimes called the Red River Rebellion, the difficulty involved a large group of French/Indian and some English/Indian people from the Red River Settlement. Known as *La Nation Metisse*, they felt no sense of unity with Canada. As early as 1849, attempted manipulation of their free trade by the Hudson's Bay Company (a practice later perpetuated by both Americans and Canadians) angered the half-breeds. Jean-Louis Riel, who originally united *La Nation Metisse*, and his son and successor Louis Riel, dreamed of an independent republican existence.

The actual rebellion began in the spring of 1885, spurred by governmental lack of concern for the half-blood's legitimate grievances. Louis Riel, by now somewhat mentally unbalanced, had moved to Montana and had become an American citizen. Nevertheless, he responded to the call of his people, returning to Canada to lead the uprising. Police were routed at Duck Lake on March 26, 1885, followed by small Indian massacres and sacking of nearby posts and settlements.

Some 8,000 troops were brought in, over the just-opened route of the C.P.R., under the direction of the brilliant American construction engineer and railroad operative, Sir William Van Horne. Riel surrendered in May, but a rebel contingent following Gabriel Dumont fought even longer. For his part in the Rebellion, Louis Riel was hanged at Regina, Saskatchewan, November 16, 1885.

The Walsh family drifted on into the province of Alberta. Apparently liking what they found there, they took up homesteads Northwest of Calgary and West of Crossfield, near what was later known as Sampsonton and ultimately became Madden.

Bernie's parents, Richard and Laura Walsh.

About 1889, while working as a butcher in nearby Banff, Richard met a lovely young woman, Laura May Wilson, who had come from Bass River near Frederickton, New Brunswick to visit her aunt, Mrs. Kate McNulty. A courtship ensued. Laura took employment with the aunt for about a year and the couple were married at Banff, April 30, 1891. Richard was 28 and Laura was 23.

Following their marriage the young couple moved to his father's homestead and were living there when their first child arrived, November 27, 1891. The baby daughter, delivered by her proud grandmother Walsh, was named Bernice.

This happy event marked the first birth of a White child North of the Bow River. The area was only sparsely settled by Indians, and just one

Three Walsh girls, Bernie at right, Grace in center, and Mary at left.

other White family lived in the 40 intervening miles between the Walsh holdings and the settlement of Calgary.

Unmindful of her distinction, the sturdy little girl flourished under the loving care of parents, grandparents and an attentive Uncle Jim, and within 11 months and 2 weeks was joined by a sister, Mary. Within another two years one more sister, Grace, arrived. All three were delivered without the assistance of a doctor.

Bernice, fondly known to family and friends simply as Bernie, had a happy childhood, but shunned the traditional play of little girls, preferring the company of all kinds of pets and livestock.

"I remember Mother giving me my China doll when I was about three," she said, "and although I always kept it, I don't think I played with it much. I would save all the big, brown paper wrappers that came on parcels. On stormy days when I could not go outside, I drew on them and planned a ranch setup. I rarely played with dolls, as my chief interest was always outside."

By the time Bernie was four years old and had aquired three siblings, including her first brother, Hiriam, her father returned to the butcher trade, taking a job with the Pat Burns Packing Company.

Pat Burns, often referred to as "Canada's Cattle King" was a very successful emigrant who accumulated large holdings and engaged in all facets of the beef trade across Canada, from breeding to table. An institution in the land, Burns was first to supply beef to the Klondike during the fabled gold rush. He was also one of the legendary "Big Four" who financed the original Calgary Stampede in 1912, as well as the second Calgary Stampede in 1919. Today, he would be called an entrepreneur.

Upon taking the job with Burns, for whom he had worked a few years earlier in Banff, Richard Walsh moved his family from the Alberta prairie homestead to Rossland, British Columbia. That is, all but Bernie.

"Grandmother wouldn't let me go. She needed me to help her. And I didn't want to go to town anyway," Bernie later recalled.

Both Richard Walsh and his brother Jim rode in the last roundup on the Beaver Dam, held in 1904, covering the range from the Bow River north to Beaver Dam. Richard Walsh is the eighth mounted man from the right, and Jim Walsh riding "Old Stray" is tenth from the right. Next left of Jim is Tom Morley. Other identified cowboys include Hector McKinsie, third mounted man from right, and Shorty Nyer, sixth mounted man from right.

2 Education

As part of a pioneering family, Bernie had many things to learn. She also had excellent teachers.

"Grandmother Walsh taught me to read and write. She taught me to hand sew, to crochet and knit, and also how to help with the housework. All our clothes were handmade, completely hand sewn, no sewing machines. Grandmother was pretty fast at it, and they were better than any store-bought ones.

"Grandmother was a wonderful Christian person. No one in the family except Uncle Jim ever said a cuss word. Nobody smoked, or used tobacco of any kind.

"Grandmother's house became my home, and I grew up quite independent, with no other children to play with, just horses, dogs and cats. Very early in life I learned to love animals," Bernie explained.

"I can well remember Indians coming close by our house, traveling from one reservation to another. Our only means of travel was by wagon or on horseback, and my elders said I could ride anybody's broke saddle horse by the time I was three years of age.

"Grandad Walsh taught me how to do outside work and ranch chores. He was a carpenter. I learned to carpenter when I was knee high to a duck, and it helped me most all of my life.

"Uncle Jim taught me to ride. At six, he said I was a top cowboy. He was always awfully good to me. He made a tomboy out of me, but I've never been sorry. Sometimes, when he'd tell me to do something, Grandmother would say, "She can't. She's too little."

"But Uncle Jim would say, 'You can do anything. Go do it.' "

After a few years the Richard Walsh family returned to Alberta. As Bernie recalled, "By the time I was nine years old my parents had moved back to the country, to my Dad's homestead, just a half-mile South. They built a log house there, and I helped shingle it. It was real fun to go down and play with the other children, two boys and the two girls, but I never stayed overnight."

During the four or five years the Walsh family lived away from the homestead, they lost three children. Richard Edwin, who lived less than a month, died in September, 1897. Alice Alberta was born on September 7 and died on October 3, 1898. Arthur James was born on October 3, 1899 and died July 27, 1900. Pioneers, though, could not look back, but must always look ahead. Richard Walsh looked to the education of his living children.

"By that time we had a very well-educated neighbor lady, Miss Stella Adams," Bernie recalled. "She was a school teacher as well as a fine artist. Dad hired her for the winter, to come over and teach the four of us in the little log bunkhouse on his homestead. I was the only one who had to go any distance to school, and then just the half-mile from Grandmother's house."

As well as Bernie and Mary could recall, some seventy years later, this was where they received their first-grade education.

"After school began," Bernie remembered, "Miss Adams told Mother I should have some paints. When I had finished my assigments I was always drawing. Sometimes, when I was at her house, Miss Adams would let me use her paints. I always loved drawing and painting."

The year following this home-school experience, the eldest Walsh children were sent into the community of Didsbury, Alberta, where they boarded with the Hunsperger family and attended school, in what was probably the second grade for both Bernie and Mary. Within the next year or so their father took another butcher's job for Pat Burns, this time in Calgary. While living there they attended school, probably in the third grade.

A humorous childhood incident Bernie recalls from that winter was not so funny to Mary, who sustained some broken ribs as a result.

"We had to walk a mile to school, and had to go down past the police barracks," Bernie said. "The kids always said there were ghosts in the police barracks. Well, I was scared of ghosts, so we'd always run by there.

"We lived in a frame house, but upstairs, where we girls slept, there was a big ridgelog brace that ran clear across the floor. We had a friend, Jessie Stokes, over for the night, and she and Mary and I were all sleeping in the one bed. Mother called us in the morning, to get up and get

Young horsewoman, Bernie Walsh.

ready for school. We were being silly, and pretty soon I said, 'We better get up and go, or she'll be up here, mad.'

"There was a pull-up door, and on the stairs going down Mother had lined up all her plants, where it would be warm for them. Well, Mary was already up and across that log, and Jesse was going, when I said, 'There's a ghost!' Then I flew past both of them as hard as I could run. Of course I scared them—even scared myself! We all jumped down from the trap door, knocking down all Mother's plants, and Mary got some broken ribs in the fall."

As time passed more people from the United States began moving to Canada to homestead. This necessitated the construction and opening of a public school, in the community of Beaver Dam, some two and one half miles from the Walsh homes. Teachers Bernie remembered there included a Mrs. Norton and a Mr. McCrimmon.

Bernie nearly always walked to and from the Beaver Dam school ("rain, shine or snow," as she put it) along with her siblings. She later recalled that it was sometimes as cold as 20 degrees below zero and the snow was often deep as they made this trek. Occasionally, if the weather was really severe, their father would take them to school in the sleigh.

Sometimes they rode horseback, keeping their horses in a barn during the day. When they did this, the noon hour would be spent riding horses a quarter of a mile to the stream to water them, an occasion for much fun and probably plenty of racing. This was mostly after Bernie quit school, however.

Her recollections of riding horseback to school involved a noon hour job. She said, "I remember one winter Uncle Jim had cattle down on his homestead, about three miles away. I rode to school, and then had to ride on over there and feed the cattle for him at noon. He'd haul hay over there with the hayrack and when we weren't in school we'd tie our sleds on behind and he'd pull us.

"One day, when Grandfather Walsh was driving, Mary's sled hit a bump or something and tipped over. Her leg was caught in behind the rope and it was dragging her. Grandfather couldn't hear, so I couldn't get him to stop and I couldn't run fast enough to catch him. All I could do was try to keep up with Mary and get her out of the rope. She was dragged quite a ways, but she finally got loose."

Along with her formal schooling, Bernie's agrarian education was also progressing rapidly.

"I drove a team before I could even sit on the seat—had to stand down in front of it. At 12 years of age I was, as the men put it, 'making a hand' with the work we had to do. I ploughed fields in the spring, working six head of horses on a two-furrow gang plow, and I also helped with the haying," she later recalled.

All this outdoor work was done in a skirt. "I never owned a pair of overalls 'till I started ranching on my own," Bernie recalled. "I always wore riding skirts, and had a pretty one for Sunday's."

Around this time, Richard and Jim Walsh aquired a butcher shop in the community of Crossfield, located on a new railroad some 12 miles East of their land.

"After that I just seemed to fall into the job of looking after the ranch," Bernie remembered. "Dad kept a hired man but he always gave me the outline of what to do each week and I got along with that real well. I feel that having to accept serious responsibility at that young age has always been a boon to me.

"Sometimes we had two hired men in haying season, and my sister Mary and I both helped. When we were 15 or 16 we made a slothe [*sweep*] to load and unload. It had a large slide. We had to drive the horses up to raise it, and when the hay was at the top it would fall on the stack. In the winter Dad fed a car load of steers for beef, all of which helped me to learn the trade."

By the time she reached the 7th grade Bernie decided she had enough to do without going to school any longer.

"I was already staying home two days a week to help Dad and my sister Mary helped Mother. She was a good nurse and good at taking care of the kids. Growing up, she was my best friend.

"By this time, Angus and Harold were in school too, and we had to practically pack them. They didn't want to go, of course, and they'd cry and bawl and we'd have to carry them half the way. So I just decided I would quit and start taking the rest of the kids to school with the driving team. I had started breaking horses, so that was a good job for them, going to school and back through the snow twice a day."

As mentioned earlier, Bernie's playmates and associates in her early years had been animals, among them the fine Clydesdale horses her father and Grandfather Walsh bred to work and to sell.

"As soon as the geldings were broke to work, they'd sell for good money. Because of that, we ended up doing our own work with the mares. The colts would be shut in the barn during the daytime while the mares were being used, and I got to hanging around down there with them. We were soon friends, and before long I got halters on some of them. I learned to halter-break them and it just went from there. Nobody ever taught me how to break horses, I just figured it out.

"Even though Uncle Jim had made a tomboy out of me, he bought me a fine sidesaddle. I got bucked off a couple of times riding it, so I threw it in the oat barrel and decided I'd ride astride, like the men."

Bernie working in the Alberta hayfield as a young woman.

In spite of her vigorous outdoor activity, Bernie's mother and grandmother saw to it that she was also educated in more feminine pursuits. A lovely embroidered runner she made under their tutelage while in her teen's won a blue ribbon at the Calgary fair. That recollection always brought a chuckle from Bernie.

"None of the girls who knew me could believe it was **my** work winning the prize. They said, 'Bernie Walsh? There must be a mistake! Why, all she knows how to do is ride horses like the boys.' So, I sure surprised them," she would say with a hearty laugh.

One winter Bernie even forsook the home place to work in the dressmaking department of the Hudson's Bay Store in Calgary. There, she learned the art of dressmaking.

"I made some dresses for neighbor ladies without patterns after that," she remembered.

Some practical experience she received in another line of work probably didn't please her mother and grandmother so much, but it may have stood her in equally good stead in later years.

She explained, "They built a new log barn at Grandfather Walsh's, and of course there were cracks of various widths between the logs, where the wind would whistle through. He wanted it tight, to protect the livestock during the cold Alberta winters, so he said, 'Bernie, we're going to stucco the new barn inside. Will you help me?'

"I was always in for any work, and learning new things, so I said I sure would. I wondered what we were going to stucco it with, and Grandfather said we'd use the most reasonable, plentiful and closely available commodity we had.

"I had no idea fresh cow manure would work so well! Grandfather taught me the proper way to stucco, and how to use a trowel and work it tight into the cracks, and we really got that barn sealed up. The soft manure dried down hard on those inside barn walls, and it lasted a surprisingly long time."

When Bernie was fourteen years old her Grandmother Walsh died, and she moved back to her parent's home.

*This lovely young woman
did all that?!*

3 Good Times

W ith the advent of numerous neighbors to the area, more social events were held and many good times were enjoyed by the young folk. One favorite winter pastime was ice skating. Bernie's first memories of skating parties were on Beaver Dam Creek, which crossed the Walsh property. She also recalled one day when it was not quite so enjoyable.

"We were skating down the creek, and it was real crooked. You couldn't see what was coming very far ahead. We came to a place where it really narrowed down and there was a riffle. We fell through the thin ice and nearly froze to death going home. It was way below zero."

Ready to ride, Bernie at right, Mary at left.

Another time, sister Mary had an unpleasant encounter on the winding creek. "She was skating along just to beat the band and all of a sudden here was a loose wire strung across the creek. It gave a little and when it came tight it just catapaulted her back up the creek about twenty feet!"

Later, Merton's Coulee on a nearby lake became a favored spot for skating parties. "We'd have a big bonfire, and lots of fun. Old Jim Briggs was a bachelor neigbor who lived not far away, and he'd always come to the skating parties, just to be around the girls," Bernie remembers with a giggle. "One time the funniest thing happened. You know, we didn't want him there anyway, and he was out on the ice in his usual stance, kind of humped over with his hands in his pockets. He had a big grin on his face watching the girls. Clarence and Lloyd Havens were pulling three of us on a sled. Somehow, when they skated past him, the sled slid over and caught the runner of his skate. His feet flew up — oh, he went as high as the ceiling!"

Another funny incident related to the skating parties involved Tillie Rock, a schoolmate that Bernie described as "kind of backward."

"She was always in the way. She couldn't skate, couldn't dance, couldn't do anything. Anyhow, Clarence and Jess Havens were pull-

Loris and Earl McLaughlin, the homesteading brothers. Loris was Bernie's "first boyfriend."

ing her and her skate caught in the hem of her dress. She just turned a somersault, and that skate just went 'bzzzt'— cut the hem right out of her dress!"

One young man with whom Bernie came in contact through these social activities was Loris McLaughlin. He and his brother Earl had homesteads near the Walsh place. Loris worked on a neighboring ranch, and Earl worked for Bernie's father and grandfather.

The legendary Cupid must have been hovering near, because the two became quite close. "I fell in love with him when I was 12," Bernie would laugh, and she ever afterward referred to him as "my first boyfriend." However, he moved to the United States about 1905, and she didn't know if she'd ever see him again.

"I just grew up with him, and didn't take him so seriously until he left. He was gone for seven years. He never wrote and I didn't either. He did send a card once, but because he didn't send a letter, I didn't answer."

Summertime social pleasures included community picnics, which were always accompanied by a variety of sporting activities. One of the favorites was horse racing, and it wasn't long until Bernie's superior abilities in the saddle made her a popular choice as jockey.

Her blue eyes always sparkled as she'd reminisce, "I got to riding race horses and made myself quite a bit of spending money."

Bernie said one feature race was always a "Free For All," and by watching it you could see which horses were really the fastest at that particular gathering. Many owners wanted Bernie to ride for them in the Ladies Race or relay events.

Using her quick, keen mind she said, "I'd never promise to ride anyone's horses until I'd watch the Free For All. I'd find out whose string of horses was fastest, and then I'd go tell them I'd ride for them that day. That made it easy to win, and I made more money that way."

Mr. Walsh kept a tight rein on his accomplished daughter, however, and was ever mindful of preserving her innocence and femininity.

"Dad wouldn't let me rodeo," Bernie remembered, somewhat regretfully. "I could have won the relay race at the Calgary Stampede in 1912. I was there, anyway, to ride in the parade, but Dad said rodeos were too rough a place for a lady. I never found it that way. I've never been offered a cigarette or a drink of whiskey around a rodeo."

The money Bernie won riding race horses went to pay for a fine saddle, which she continued to ride throughout her lifetime.

Bernie on one of her racing mounts, at probably 17 or 18 years of age.

4   Calgary Adventure

I t was in April of 1911 that Bernie unexpectedly walked into one of the most memorable adventures of her lifetime.

In her words: "My sister Mary, my Dad and I went to Calgary to the Horse Show. We were taking it all in and enjoying everything when we were approached by Mr. D.P. Mc Donald, a neighbor who lived some 40 miles from us.

"He had known me all my life and thought I was a good rider. He told me he was looking for someone to ride his fine jumping horse, Smokey, in the high jump contest that night. I wondered why he didn't already have a rider, and then he explained that the man who'd trained Smokey was refusing to ride him. He'd already tried out two male jockeys, and Smokey had thrown them both off.

"After hearing all that, my Dad and all my friends tried to discourage me from accepting the job. I didn't have much time to decide, because the contest was coming up that very evening. I thought it over and said, 'Well, it couldn't hurt much to get throwed off in that soft sawdust ring, so I'll ride him.' "

The matter settled, it was time for a trial run, so Mc. Donald escorted the group to an area "out behind the Calgary stadium." Bernie never forgot the struggle she had then.

"I wore a ladies divided skirt and Smokey had never been ridden by a lady, so I had quite a time even getting up to him. After a lot of persuasion I finally got on him, and then he acted pretty nice. I rode him around for nearly an hour, just getting used to him and letting him get used to me. Then we went inside the stadium, and I jumped him only once, over about a four-foot jump. He acted like he enjoyed it."

Then came a time of anticipation and waiting, because the Men's High Jump class was not on the program until 10 pm. Bernie remem-

Over the top and down, effortlessly. A shot from the Alberta Industrial Exhibition, 1911, where Bernie and Smokey established the world record.

bered, "I had never seen the horse until that day, and I'd never tried a high jump. But Smokey was a cowhorse, and I decided to just ride him like one, with one hand. I figured that was what had caused him to throw the jockeys—they were trying to ride him two-handed."

Bernie always spoke of riding Smokey in that famous contest like it was commonplace and involved no stress for her. The amazing photo taken during competition would seem to confirm that attitude. It shows her soaring over one of the brush and pole jumps with a smile on her face, tailored riding habit and prim little hat looking as if she'd just stepped out of a band box, reins gripped deftly in her gloved left hand, right hand holding the riding crop to the rear in readiness. The photo will cause the most experienced equestrian to gasp in unbelief, and then probably shudder.

Smokey's ears are up, his body in proper jumping form, but Bernie's hold on the reins is very short, necessitating the extension of her left arm far up his neck. This, in company with the riding crop poised over his rump, shows Bernie knew horses and operated with the foresight of a winner, being well-prepared for any effort on Smokey's part to avoid going over the jump.

However, it placed her, riding a two-pound jockey saddle (which might be compared to sitting on a pancake for the amount of stability it would lend a rider), in a most unusual, totally erect and almost spread-eagle position. Had she not posessed an amazing balance born only of untold hours in the saddle, the terrific power of the big horse thrusting up and over the jump and the shock of landing again would have sent her hurtling through the air. The balance necessary for such a feat excels that of a trick rider executing the most difficult of no-hands movements such as the liberty stand.

Normally, for such high jumps, a rider's body bends forward from the hips, nearly level with the horse's neck. The reins are held in two hands, low and very near the neck, giving horse and rider a oneness of stability and avoiding most of the natural resistance, as with the aerodynamic design of an airplane. Even so, any good rider will tell you it's no snap to clear a six foot two inch barricade!

Apparently oblivious to such things, Bernice summed up the evening by saying, "Anyhow, we made it and our last jump was six feet, two inches. That was about 11:30 pm. The event was over and they said we had won. It was quite a surprise for me!"

Surprising as it may have been to Bernie, it also surprised and no doubt chagrined a lot of horsemen. In addition to the fact that the rider was a slip of a young ranch girl, Smokey was not a highly pedigreed show horse.

"He was pretty well bred, but not much to look at," Bernie would chuckle. "A dirty brown color. He was quite an unusual horse though, and had lots of sense, if you could get him to use it. That first time we won the high jump it was a World's Record and they gave me a gold medal watch. The other two times I rode him, I got paid for it."

As you learned from that statement, there were other victories in store for Bernie and Smokey. Following their initial win in April, they teamed up again at the July fair and repeated their triumph over the men in open high jump. That was more than male vanity could allow, and steps were taken to prevent further humiliation.

As Bernie explained, "The next Spring Horse Show they ruled me out, and instead put on a ladies high jump, limiting the height to five feet. All the other ladies rode sidesaddle and no one could make the five feet, so Smokey and I won for the third time."

That feat made the Calgary newspapers. A yellowed clipping was saved over the years among Bernie's things, not from the Calgary paper, but apparently from a home-town publication. It quoted the Calgary story, which included some details Bernie never mentioned. Perhaps they are simply the literary embellishments of a writer uneducated in equitation, perhaps they are true. At any rate, the entire clipping reads:

"MISS WALSH'S SUCCESS—We are sorry not to be able to procure the cuts of Miss Walsh on 'Smokey.' Evidently the people of Calgary are too busy making money to even acknowledge the letters which we wrote regarding the cuts. However it is too good to be allowed to pass without due notice. Cut it out and paste it in your scrap book. We may never have such honors thrust upon us again. It will be remembered that Miss Walsh last year took this headstrong horse in hand after he had succeeded in throwing his regular rider and put him over a 6 ft. 2 in. hurdle, thereby beating the world's record for an amateur lady rider. Miss Walsh and her mount at once became famous all over Canada and the United States.

"Here is what the Albertan had to say about the matter.

"Three thousand spectators who remained at the Horse Show until well after 12 o'clock last night were thrilled when Miss Walsh on 'Smokey' world's record breaker, and winner of the lady amateur high jump of last year, captured the first place again. The winning of Miss Walsh and her game little horse was not without its spectacular and dangerous features. When the animal cleared the jump and raced madly from the end of the arena, he was only brought to a standstill by the end gates of the ring.

" 'The horse appeared nervous at the start and ran away with the rider on three occasions during the course of the event. The first time he became uncontrollable the spectators did not realize the danger until they heard the pretty daughter of the Carstairs rancher cry, 'He is running away.'

" 'The lives of the spectators at the end of the ring were in danger for it looked as though 'Smokey' was going to clear the end fence and bolt out of the building. But Miss Walsh showed her pluck when she quieted the horse and returned to make him take the four foot barrier. At the four foot eight mark 'Smokey' again got away and putting his head down went over the barrier, knocking the top rail off.

" 'Miss Walsh's riding was superb. Gradually all but one horse, Sioux, ridden by Miss Minnie Gardiner, were eliminated. The barrier was placed at five feet, the highest mark allowed by the judges because of fear of an accident.

" 'Miss Walsh was greeted by a roar of applause as she rode into the ring. Twice the top bar was kicked off as Smokey went over. Then on the third and last try, the pony seemingly maddened by his unsuccessful efforts put his head down and made a brave dash for the bars. The spectators held their breath. He cleared by inches and continued his rush right to the end of the rink, where he was stopped by the fence and spectators.

" 'Sioux failed to clear the five foot barrier by a fraction of an inch. On form Sioux would have won. His take off was graceful and according to the ethics of all hunting books, but the cow horse with an uncertain pedigree again proved the winner and Miss Walsh was the heroine of the evening.' "

Mr. D.P. McDonald, owner of Smokey, lived at Cochrane, Alberta, where he owned a large ranch. His property included the townsite, and his grandson still lives there. Cochrane was one community which always held the summer rodeos Bernie loved.

Bernie and Smokey the cowhorse, with which she broke the Women's Amateur World Record in high jumping at Calgary in the spring of 1911. These photos were probably taken at the Calgary fair that fall, when the duo again won the Men's High Jumping division. (See two photos on the next page also.)

5 Marriage

About three months after Bernie's third and final jumping victory on her cowhorse pal, Smokey, she came to another of the most important events in her life. She told it like this.

"In July of 1912, I was riding horseback into Carstairs, a little town 20 miles north. We did not have a telephone in our community yet, and I needed to call in an entry for two races the next day. So I stopped at Jim Banta's place to use the telephone. I was totally amazed and flustered when my first boyfriend, Loris McLaughlin, came to the door. He had been gone to Oklahoma for seven years."

As Loris hastily explained, Banta's wife had become quite ill and he was called away from the ranch to accompany her for medical care. Because Loris McLaughlin had worked for him before and was a capable, trustworthy young man who understood the ranching business and the country, Banta phoned Oklahoma, requesting him to come immediately and take over the cattle, sheep, and farming duties on his place.

Loris had come as quickly as possible, and now he and Bernie suddenly found themselves face to face.

After making her phone call, she proceeded to resume her journey to Carstairs.

"Loris suggested riding into Carstairs with me, or at least part way, and I had to confess to him that I was engaged. He said, 'You have nothing on me. I am, too.' But it all worked out OK for us."

The look on Bernie's face and the depth of expression in her eyes as she made that last statement said much more than the words which came from her lips. She would just go on to tell, matter-of-factly that she married Loris in 1913.

Between the lines, one could hardly help understanding that the depth of feeling Loris and Bernie had for one another from the time

𝔐arriage 𝔠ertificate

What God Hath Joined Together
Let Not Man Put Asunder

Autographs of Gr...

Witnesses: Albert Hiram W...
Mary Walsh
Richard Wal...
Laura Wals...
Grace Walsh
Harold Walsh
Angus Walsh
Martha Walsh
Elsie Walsh
James Walsh
Jessie Walsh
Albert J Walsh
Elizabeth Garwood

The marriage certificate

Wedding day, March 22, 1913, Loris and Bernie McLaughlin.

of their first acquaintance as mere children had been the force which kept both of them, at better than twenty years of age, from having turned their engagements into marriages. Even though they had not seen one another for seven years, their relationship picked up immediately upon that chance meeting in July of 1912.

"I'd never quit looking for him to come back," Bernice shyly confided.

With her beauty, charm, and ability, Bernie had not been without suitors in Loris' absence. The man she was engaged to was Harry Linsey, whom she said was ten years older than her. They were good friends, but Bernie said she felt more like he was her uncle.

"He was very good to me, and offered me a lot to marry him," she remembered, "but he wasn't as good-looking as Loris.

"If I had ever married him I'd have blamed my mother for it. Dad didn't like livestock, but Mother did. Every time I'd get in trouble over the amount of stock I had, Harry would get me out of it. When Loris, my real dream, came back and I broke our engagement, Harry wasn't surprised, just disappointed."

The wedding was held in Sampsonton, Alberta on March 22, 1913, with Rex Brown officiating. Bernie's brother Hiriam and sister Mary served as witnesses, and there were 11 other guests, 10 of them members of the Walsh family.

Bernie was lovely in a long sleeved, ankle length gown of white silk, trimmed with satin and intricate beadwork, handmade by a friend, Mrs. Garwood. Her high-heeled slippers were also satin – size 4! She wore an elegant beaded headdress with a sheer veil that trailed down her back to below her knees.

Resplendent in a three-piece suit, the groom chose a shirt with French cuffs, and a bow tie. His shoes for the occasion sported black patent leather toes.

A wedding supper was held, and the traditional British wedding cake, a rich fruitcake, was served. The beautifully decorated, three tiered cake was baked and decorated by the friend who made the wedding dress, Mrs. Garwood.

Loris McLaughlin was an international man. Born in Decator County, Iowa, he and a brother, Earl had gone to Canada and filed on homesteads. That Canadian residency was followed by the seven years back in the States, and now he was once again living in Canada.

In Bernie's eyes, he was perfect. "Loris was outgoing, a good mixer," she said.

After marrying Bernie, he continued to work in Alberta. She remembers, "I went right on helping with the cowboy work when I had time. I also had two hired men to cook for as well as two telephones to answer, and they would not let us connect them. People would often call asking us to phone and tell someone on the North line something. We'd have to call and relay the message and then call them back. That was a headache!

"We lived there two years and by then our son, Stanley, had arrived. Loris picked his name, after a neighbor child Stanley Gaetson. They were a German family, and he was quite a little boy, so polite and nice.

"By this time the rancher's wife had regained her health and he really wanted the ranch back, so we sold him our stock and lease. We were planning to move up into the Peace River country, some 500 miles on North. While talking it over Loris suggested maybe we should go back down to Cherokee, Oklahoma and visit his aged parents before we moved farther away, so they could meet me and Stanley. Also, his favorite brother Earl had gone back to the States."

The three-tiered wedding cake baked by Mrs. Garwood for Loris and Bernie. It was the English and Canadian traditional wedding cake, a very rich fruitcake. Wanda recalls that her mother saved the small top layer, and that she and Stanley were allowed to eat some of it when they were quite small.

Therefore, the little family took the train and journeyed from Alberta to Oklahoma for a visit over the Christmas holiday. As it happened, Earl, who'd been cowboying in Wyoming, was also home to visit.

Earl told Loris he had taken a liking to some New Mexico country he'd passed through on his homeward trip. Stopping off there for a few weeks, he wound up filing on a 320 acre homestead.

"Right after Christmas, Loris went with Earl on the train to see the New Mexico country," Bernie said. "Loris liked the looks of it, too, and thought it would be a good way for us to get some land. But he said he wouldn't want to do it unless I liked it, too. Well, I always did want a little ranch somewhere, so we decided to buy a team and make the journey with Earl from the elder McLaughlin's place in Oklahoma to his New Mexico homestead.

Stanley McLaughlin and his proud parents at the Banta place in Canada.

Another shot of Stanley and Loris, dressed to go for a Sunday drive from the Banta place. Note the team tied to the fence in readiness.

The visiting Canadian, Stanley takes a look at Grandma McLaughlin's porch in Oklahoma the day after arriving there.

6 Homesteading

"**G**etting a saddle horse and team and fixing up a covered wagon kept us real busy until the first of April. Stanley was only a year old and Loris thought I should take him and go on the train, as it might be hard on us to make the trip by wagon. But not me. I wanted us all to go together. We started on the tenth of April, 1916.

"The weather was nice for three days, and we enjoyed the trip very much. Then we ran into snow for two days, but we were comfortable, although we did have to stop for half a day at Guymon, Oklahoma. We made the 300 mile journey in 11 days and landed at Earl's homestead safe and sound.

"He had a little dugout so we could cook inside, but we used our wagons to sleep in. The men did most of the cooking, as Stanley was just the right age that it kept me busy trying to keep him off the dirt floor. After spending a couple of weeks at Earl's, Loris and I drove our wagon the 35 miles into the town of Clayton, New Mexico, to see what we could find.

"The land agent was Mr. Ira Pennington, and he took us in his car (which was quite a treat!) out to look at a place called Yates. We didn't like it there, so we came back to Clayton and he took us out North of Moses in the real rough country. That didn't look good to us either.

"After checking out those possibilities and spending another few days in Clayton, we went back to Earl's. About all he'd had time to accomplish was fencing the property, so Loris helped him build a little corral for the horses. Then they borrowed an extra plow and he helped break up a patch of ground so Earl could get a crop started.

"Meanwhile, we kept looking for land of our own. We finally found a half section 2 1/2 miles Southeast of Cuates that a Mr. Yates wanted to relinquish. It had a two-wire fence and a dugout that had caved in. It was the only place we'd seen that we liked, but they were asking $1100 for it. After a good bit of consideration, we decided to take it."

All of this took up still more time, and necessitated yet another trip to Clayton in the wagon. Bernice remembers, "Stanley and I went along and stayed several days with Mr. and Mrs. Watkins. He worked at the railroad station and she ran a little boarding house. I learned to love her, and several others I met at that time.

The covered wagons used for the trip from Cherokee, Oklahoma, to the new home in New Mexico.

"Loris had to take out his Declaration of Intention to become a U.S. Citizen before he could re-file on the 320 acres of land," she explained.

"There was a bad hill about twelve miles North of Clayton, and as we started down it on our trip home one of the mares got to fighting the britchen harness and kicking. I said, "Let me out, I'll carry Stanley down here.""

"Loris sure kidded me about that. He said, 'That is the first time I ever saw you afraid of anything!'

"Our new property was six miles East of Earl's place. We unloaded the over-jett from the wagon, bought a tent, and set up housekeeping. Within a week we brought in a good well at a depth of 114', so Loris took Earl's wagon to Clayton to get a windmill and lumber to build a tower. Earl helped us quite a lot and soon we had the mill up and were getting lots of water.

"Loris got us a plow and fenced a little spot for a garden in June. I just couldn't stand to see water going to waste, so I planted seed onions, beets, peas, and beans. Believe it or not, I had a wonderful little garden when fall came!"

After the water situation had been attended, thoughts turned to shelter. The McLaughlin's decided to utilize the raw materials readily available from a quarry five miles away. They planned a two-story stone home 12' by 24'. The rock had to be quarried and hauled in with teams, so the work went rather slowly. Bill Moore, a close neighbor of Earls, brought his team and wagon and helped them.

Three neighbors who knew stone masonry were hired to lay up the outside walls of the home, which would have a kitchen and living room on the ground level and two bedrooms upstairs. Once the walls were up, lumber was needed for joists, flooring, roofing and to install the door and window facings. Bernice vividly remembers Loris going into town for those supplies.

"Loris and Delbert Begley took two teams and wagons to Clayton for the lumber. That was the 10th of August, and it had been a very dry summer. After the men left it was mail time at Cuates, so I took the spare team and another wagon we'd bought and drove the 2 1/2 miles for the mail. It began to rain, and Stanley (who was about 21 months old) and I got a good soaking before we got home.

"We put the team away and then got in the tent and had a good drink of hot tea. I fixed us some supper and after we ate we crawled out of

Bernice, Stanley and Wanda in front of their New Mexico home.

the tent into the over-jett and went to bed. It simply poured all night long, with lots of thunder and lightning. I sure didn't sleep. The next morning it was still pouring, so we stayed in bed until we got hungry.

"When I did get up and try to get inside the tent I thought I'd never get those wet tent ropes untied. They were set up hard as iron and I got a good wetting while working at them. But I finally wriggled them loose, got inside and fixed us some breakfast. It continued to rain all that day and night, but at least the lightning had stopped, so it wasn't quite so bad.

"By the third day the weather had cleared, but I knew the men could never start out from Clayton until the roads dried up. That afternoon Earl rode over and brought us some roasting ears. It brightened our situation a good deal just to see him and have someone to talk to, and he also assured me that the men should be able to make it home by the end of the week. He was right. They'd left Monday morning, and they made it in late Friday night."

It had now been four and a half months since the little family drove away from the elder McLaughlin's home in Oklahoma, and Bernice was still a long way from having a real house. Yet she never spoke of this time as having been hard or trying. Rather, it was part of a great and exciting adventure, the establishment of their very own home and the beginning of the ranch she'd always hoped for.

It became known as the Triple Link Ranch, taking the name from Loris' brand. He was a member of the International Order of Odd Fellows, whose emblem is three connected chain links, in a horizontal format. He registered the emblem vertically as his brand, to be used on the left shoulder.

"We got the roof on the house and moved in with the springs and mattress on the floor the first of October. At that time we made another trip to Clayton to get a better cook stove, a heating stove, bedstead and other essentials.

"On the 7th of December our little girl, Wanda, arrived," Bernice said, in her matter-of-fact way. "A near neighbor, Mrs. Begley, had offered to come when we called her, so another little one arrived without a doctor. But we got along just fine. Loris again chose the name, this time after a little girl we'd met in Oklahoma.

"I was pretty busy the next summer with the two little ones, but I still helped outside all I could, taking the kiddies along. We had a fair little crop that year.

"That fall, in November, I was called on to help deliver a baby. I had helped Mrs. Begley once before, so she came by and got me, and had me take over. I was willing to try, and we got through with no trouble. Loris kept the children that night, and the next day he called me 'Doctor'.

"We had a crop the next year, too, enough that we could feed our horses and cows, as well as a few beans. It was quite interesting to me to learn the different ways of farming. It had all been flat farming in Canada, but we soon learned the new way." [*Reference to the accepted practices of contouring and terracing.*]

Posing by their new stone home on the homestead. Earl and Stanley at left, Loris and baby Wanda at right.

7   Tragedy

Loris and Bernice McLaughlin were both well-fitted for their roles as prairie pioneers, knowing and loving livestock and the agricultural pursuits necessary to survival in a barren and rugged land. They had each other and a healthy 4 1/2-year-old son and a 2 1/2-year-old daughter. They had a snug and sturdy, if small, home, land enough to begin with, and the dream of eventually building a sizable ranch. They had some farming equipment, three cows and five horses (two work teams and a saddle horse). They had many good friends and congenial neighbors. They were still fairly young and both in excellent health. The future truly looked bright.

Bernice continues her story. "On the 18th of September, 1919, Loris was in the field cutting the maize. It started to rain hard, so he came in early. He got very wet coming in. Leaving the team harnessed in the barn, he came to the house to get a dry coat. Since it was raining so hard and the team had feed in the barn, we decided to eat supper and see if it would let up some.

"By the time we'd finished supper it was raining even harder. Loris was worried about a sow that had ten little pigs in a pen South of the corral. Saying 'I must go down and see if they are ok,' he lit a lantern and went out. It was already dark.

"It began to lightning real bad while he was checking on the pigs. As he returned, he stopped to shut a wire gate about a hundred yards in front of the house, and the loudest crash of lightning hit! I ran to the door and could see his lantern upset near the gate. Right then I felt he must have been hit.

"I told the children to stay where they were, just inside the door, and I would be right back. It sure didn't take me long to get there, but he was already lifeless and had never struggled, so I knew he had been killed instantly. I went right back to the house and got a canvas to cover him with. There was no loose stock around, and I couldn't move him anyway.

"I went back in and told the children we'd have to go over to Jake Castor's. They lived about a mile West of us. Our wagon was loaned out to another neighbor who needed it to haul wood, so all I had to drive was the sturdy stone-boat that we normally used for hauling heavy things around the place. What a blessing the team was still in the barn with the harness on!

"When we got to the Castor place, Mr. Castor didn't have a horse in the corral, so he walked another mile to get Mr. W.F. Kendrick, who had a car. They then went on over to get Earl and came back by the Post Office and got Mr. C.D. Ellis."

After driving the slow stone-boat to Castors and telling them of the tragedy, Bernice and her cold, wet, and frightened children returned alone to the homestead with the team and stone-boat. Throughout this time, Bernice exhibited the strength typical of pioneer women. She did not panic or become hysterical, but calmly made decisions as to what must be done, and then bravely carried them through. Disregarding her own feelings, she thought of her children.

"The kiddies and I had just gotten home when the four men arrived in the car. It was very hard for Stanley and Wanda to understand, as young as they were. They finally went to sleep about midnight.

"Mr. Kendrick and Mr. Ellis made a rough box out of some new 1'x12' lumber that we had, and by 11 am the next morning we were on our way to Clayton in the wagon. I had two feather beds and lots of quilts that made a good padding. The creeks had all been up and washed in at the crossings so we knew a car couldn't make it. We got to Clayton just before dark."

Even going with the team and wagon, the trip was not easy. Several of Bernice's neighbors accompanied her on horseback as far as Corrumpa Creek. There, they rode their horses back and forth across the creek several times, to settle the quicksand and make it possible to cross the wagon.

When she arrived in Clayton, the brave young widow found her burden of decision-making had only just begun.

She continued, "The funeral home did a nice job, and he looked real nice. I called Grandma and Grandpa McLaughlin at Cherokee, Oklahoma. None of us wanted to lay him away in New Mexico. Right then I didn't think I could possibly stay on."

They decided to take the body to Oklahoma for burial. Earl accompanied Bernice and the children, and they made the trip on the same train with Loris' body.

"We went to Alva, Oklahoma, and the ambulance met us there," Bernice remembered. "We stayed over there a week. Another brother, George and his wife and little boy from Lone Rock, Oregon were visiting the old folks and had planned to come and see us in a month. So, when the week was up they accompanied us back home and spent three weeks with us here.

"Earl and George had not seen each other for ten years. After they had been with us three weeks, they went back to Oklahoma and stayed another month with the folks."

Miz Mac, Stanley and Wanda.

8   Perseverance

"Every noble work is at first impossible."   Carlysle

Bernice held within her torn and broken heart and bewildered mind the conviction that she could not possibly remain on the homestead and carry on. Yet she was practical enough to push such future decisions aside and face each day, doing what must be done at the moment.

"When we got home after the funeral the neighbors all pitched in and finished cutting the crop and shocking the feed. We had a real good crop. There was corn, maize, cane and beans.

"We had planned to build a granary, in fact Loris had already purchased the lumber. In order that I would not have to sell the grain right out of the field, Mr. Kendrick helped us build it.

"It sure was the right thing to do, as grain prices were nearly double by spring. That gave me a lift, and I began to look ahead and plan to stay. I liked the climate and I had real good neighbors. I have always been glad I made that decision."

Besides being a young widow with children to support, Bernice Mc Laughlin was not even a citizen of the country in which she dwelt. Nor did that country prove kindly to her.

"Since Loris was gone I knew I had to re-file on the homestead. Before I could do that I had to apply for my declaration to become a United States citizen. Then I found out that the Government would not honor the time Loris had put in toward proving up on the homestead. Instead, they treated it as a relinquishment, and it took me six years to get the title."

Bernice's Certificate of Naturalization, #737399, was issued to her on November 9, 1948. It confirms that she "was naturalized by the District Court of Union County at Clayton, New Mexico on March 6, 1922."

Stanley and Wanda with baby chicks, and their faithful protector, Old Kernel. This is about the size they were when their father was killed.

Bernice's family in Canada swiftly came to her aid. "Hiriam, the oldest boy in my family, had just arrived home from serving in World War I, and he came down from Canada the first of October to be with me. He stayed until the first of April in 1920. Just before he left, my second brother Harold, who was only 19, came. He stayed three years.

"Harold never did like row farming. He was a rodeo cowboy and wanted to be at home for the Calgary Stampede, but we did enjoy having him and appreciated him staying. I traded a few calves for a second-hand car so he would be better satisfied. I also gave him half of what we had to sell, so he'd have something to go on. After the three years, I urged him to go home, because he loved rodeoing, and he was good at it."

That statement was true, not just a proud sister's opinion. Harold Walsh was also known as Harley. In a 1961 article published in the Canadian Cattleman magazine, Gordon Y. Thompson, himself a successful rodeo cowboy and acknowledged historical authority on Canadian rodeo, wrote the following:

"It was at Nanton, Alberta, in 1932 that I first saw Harley Walsh, Canadian bronc riding champion. He came out in one of his high-spurring rides to hook a spur in the halter ring of his bronc. I watched with my heart in my mouth as the horse jerked Harley from his saddle. He was saved from death by several cowboys leaping onto the horse's head until Harley's spur was freed."

*Enjoying the fruits of Bernice's labors, Stanley,
Wanda and Kernel with garden produce
alongside the house.*

Bernice continued her recollections, "During the time Harold was with us, Stanley started to school. It was called Circle Valley, and was just two miles from home. I had to put him on behind me riding the little grey saddle horse I had. Wanda was five, and sometimes she'd go along, three of us on the horse, but she preferred staying home, so she learned at an early age to wash the dishes. She could watch us for a mile going and coming, and it didn't take me long.

"One day we decided to go and visit the Moore family, who lived a half mile South of the school. So Wanda went with me, and after we left Stanley off at school we went on to Moores. Mr. Moore had a real pretty bunch of little Chester White pigs, just weaning age. I asked if he would sell me one.

"He said, 'I'll give you one, if you can carry it home on that little horse.'

"Well, I sure wanted a sow pig, so we got a heavy sack to put it in. He said Wanda could stay with them and I could come back for her, so I took my pig and started out. It was quite a show for a while, as that little horse sure tried to get out of that job, but we finally got home. I arrived back for Wanda just in time to have dinner with the Moores. They then insisted we stay and visit until time to take Stanley home from school. That little sow pig made us a lot of money.

"She raised two litters a year for five years. We had milk to feed them, so that was a help. She got so big and cranky I finally had to get rid of her, but in 1927 we raised enough pigs to buy a new Ford car.

"We raised the corn, fattened the pigs, and I made three trips to Clayton with the wagon to market. There were no trucks then."

Bernice raised and broke mules to work, and often drove them to the wagon. True to mule nature, they weren't always completely cooperative. She especially remembered one trip to town with a load of pigs. A neighbor accompanied her in the wagon. It was kind of icy, and they had to cross quite a narrow bridge with bannisters. One of the four mules in the team was a troublemaker.

Sharing some, with Uncle Harold Walsh, down from Canada.

"That silly mule was always seeing boogers. He got to shying around from the edge, and slipped on the ice. He fell so that his legs slid out under the bannister."

While the neighbor was eager to go to his rescue, Bernice understood animal nature well enough to know that Mr. Mule was about to teach himself a good lesson. She said, "Just let him figure out how to get himself out of that fix."

By the time the thoroughly frightened mule wriggled around and made it to his feet, assisted by a little dragging from the other three scared mules, he'd learned it was much healthier to tend to business and stay on his feet.

"He was a good mule from then on," Bernice laughed. "He'd been to college that day, and he never looked sideways anymore."

Bernice's brother Harold had returned to Canada in 1923. In 1925 the sixth living child in the Walsh family, Martha, made her visit to New Mexico.

"She came for her health," Bernice recalled. "She regained that in a year, but she liked it so well here that she remained three years."

The young widow lived very frugally, managing her limited funds wisely. In addition to always raising a big garden, she planted and lovingly tended peach, cherry, apple and pear trees. Harvest-time was always accompanied by lots of canning. The cattle produced milk and meat, and Bernice said she "always made the children's clothes." Through such wise stewardship she was able not only to hold the little ranch together but also to continue building it up.

Stanley, all ready for the first day of school. Wanda looked on enviously, knowing she had to stay behind.

"I eventually accumulated a little bunch of cattle, but not enough to make a living. One of my neighbors was wanting to leave the country so bad that he said he'd trade his 12 head of dairy-type cattle for a car. I didn't have any money for gas anyway, and my car was getting old, so I just traded him. I got a dozen nice young cows and heifer calves.

"Then I traded one cow that wasn't so good to another family for a new cream separator. Now, with no car and all those milk cows we really went to work. We milked 12 cows each summer until the children finished school, and we certainly were not among the unemployed. The children did lots of the chores, but they didn't mind it, and they never missed a day of school to work."

Bernice taught both Stanley and Wanda to ride, using the saddle she'd bought in Canada with her horse-racing money. "It was the only saddle we owned for years," Wanda later recalled.

When Wanda was old enough for school, both children would some-times walk the two miles. Bernice laughed, "It was mostly South, so if the wind was in the north they'd turn a tumbleweed loose and chase it all the way to school."

One school teacher, Mattie Blake, boarded at the McLaughlin home. In addition to the Circle Valley school, Stanley and Wanda also attended rural schools at Prairie Dale and Cuates.

Bernice also saw to it that her children attended Sunday School. True to her code of helping with everything, she did her part by playing for the services. She explained, "When I first came here, Marie Weiland was my neighbor. They came about a year before we did. When she was about 35 she taught herself to read music and play the piano. I learned enough from her to play for Sunday School, but never learned to read music. I played for Sunday School for three years."

In the field, Mrs. Begley and children at left, Miz Mac with Wanda and Stanley at left. Mrs. Begley was the neighbor who came when Wanda arrived, and was Miz Mac's teacher in midwifing skills.

This is Old Whitey, the little pig that rode home in a sack with Miz Mac—all grown up now and boasting ten new little pigs. Two are underneath, mostly out of sight.

Wanda on Redwing, with Uncle Earl McLaughlin.

Bernie and children, in the garden below the windmill.

9 Expansion

"I built up my cow herd until I had to lease two sections of grass. Later, in 1928, I bought 240 acres of land that had two streams of water on it, and also leased the school section just across the road from my homestead.

"I had to fence it and build a dam. That was done with the four-horse team and a frezno. I drove the team, and hired a man to run the frezno.

"After buying that land we were hit with a bad drough and one year the grasshoppers really took us. For two years I didn't even get to use the new land but had to move the cattle around wherever I could find pasture. I finally brought them home and sold them to the Government to keep them from starving to death, as two had already died. I had 80 head at the time, and didn't owe a thing on them."

Years later, Bernice's daughter Wanda recalled this vividly. She said, "They shot the cattle over in the West pasture and covered them up with a bulldozer. That was a very sad day. We kept some of the meat from the ones that were in the best condition, and canned enough meat with pressure cookers to last us for two or three years."

Bernice continued her recollections, saying, "The Government paid $12 a head for the cows and $4 for the calves. I had borrowed $3,000 to pay for the land, and the expense of moving the cattle around for two years took all the rest. The bank let me keep 15 two-year-old heifers that were calving in August. The government killed their calves [*in an effort to reduce numbers and salvage the rangeland after the prolonged drouth*] and I knew the heifers wouldn't calve the following year. Still, I thought I could at least come out with some young cows in two years.

"I also kept 20 of the big calves, and had to cut soapweeds [*yucca*] by hand for feed for them that winter. In the spring I traded the 15 steers for heifers and started over again.

*Some of the cows Miz Mac
worked so hard for.*

"I bought the tax title to yet another section of land, which had very little grass on it. That took a lot of nerve, but in two years the grass came back real good and so did cattle prices. Then I bought another section, and for several years it was hard to catch up.

"I finally sold a load of yearling steers for 40 cents a pound, and that got me out [*of debt*] again. The next year I got a chance to buy eleven head of real good registered Hereford cows. They had some age on them, running 7 to 9 years old, but I had lots of feed and took good care of them.

"The first two year's bull calves paid for the cows and I had the heifer calves left. Then I started selling off my old grade cows each fall and keeping registered heifers.

"I was able to keep the original registered cows five years, and got them sold just in time, ahead of a hard winter. But I kept the papers up and soon built back to 80 head of mother cows and got out [*of debt*] again.

"I always did a lot of farming, all with horses and mules, and I always broke my own teams to work. Most of them I also raised. I farmed 100 acres, practiced contouring, and built dams, dikes, and ditches. I raised dryland corn, cane, maize and hygrie. There was never but one year I didn't have a crop, and I didn't even raise much of a garden!

"That was during the long drouth in the Dust Bowl days of the 30's. Most of my neighbors moved out. I finally planted some rye, from seed that a neighbor gave me when he left, and it got enough moisture to come up and survive, somehow.

"The children were a lot of help and pleasure to me. We always went to Sunday school and to all the games and plays and school activities — everything going on. Sometimes we had no transportation but the

Never afraid of hard work, Miz Mac is branding here, with Mr. Chilcote holding the head and Stanley on the hind leg.

Helping the neighbors, Miz Mac does the branding at Kendrick's place.

buggy and a little team of light mules, but we got there anyway and often took the Davis children along.

"The first two years of high school Stanley and Wanda had a 40 mile trip every day, into Seneca. We saved enough to buy them a car, as there was no school bus service then. They finished high school in Clayton in 1934, and both married the next year.

"Stanley and his wife Marjorie (Tennis) lived with me on the ranch the first five years. For a time Stanley drove the school bus to Seneca. Then he went to work for Colorado Interstate Gas Company.

"Wanda married Riley Hughes. He worked in the dry cleaning business and she went to work in the Court House.

"After they both married I hired help part of the time. I also built onto the house some. I'd drawn up plans to enlarge the house years before, but I never got time to do it."

A dust storm sweeps into Clayton, NM, at 6:30 pm on May 21, 1937. The effects of this drouth put a lot of people out of the ranching business, and made times plenty hard for Miz Mac.

Several additions were made to the house over the years, with rock tie-in's being used so skillfully it's difficult to tell it wasn't all built at once. Bernice had an idea to use stucco on the outside of the final frame addition, and sculpt it to look like the native stone.

The builders told her that was impossible, so she did it herself, perhaps utilizing the skills she learned on her first "stucco" job with her grandfather Walsh in Canada. Sculpturing the wet stucco to match the native stone shapes, she then dabbed it with paint to get the proper color. To the casual observer, the entire house seems to be built of the same stone.

"I always supervised everything, and I always paid my help," Bernice declared. "Once someone said I didn't owe them anything after they'd helped me with a job and I said, 'You can't work for me for nothing!'

"One time a well-driller I'd hired asked me, 'How do you know so much about wells?'

"I said, 'If you'd paid for all the ones I have, you'd know, too!' I had five windmills and two creeks on my property, besides the five dams I put in."

Miz Mac has been working cattle on Pecos.

Miz Mac on Goldie, ready for a day's work.

Miz Mac feeding cattle with Mr. Kendrick.

The registered Herefords that helped pay off the debt. This photo was taken right after she caked them in winter.

10 The Amazing Miz Mac

Over the years it became common belief around the Clayton, New Mexico area that nothing was impossible for Miz Mac, as Bernice was fondly known far and wide. In fact, folk from the area said that as sure as anyone said something "couldn't be done," Miz Mac would do it!

And, they were right. There really wasn't much she couldn't do. Even during the years Miz Mac was rearing her children and struggling to make a living, she was called upon by neighbors for a multitude of tasks. This was probably because she had such a calm, practical approach to all situations, and was a comforting person to have around in times of trial or emergency. She also had a penchant for perseverance which was an encouragement to everyone around her.

One incident Bernice related took place while her children were still in grade school. "I was called on to help with a boy who was hurt just North of us. He was 14 years old, and his horse had fallen on him. He lived through the night, but died the next day. I had to lay him out, and we fixed his body to be taken into Clayton in a car."

The Holy Bible, in which Miz Mac was a firm believer, teaches in II Corinthians 1:3 & 4, ". . .the God of all comfort. . .comforts us in all our troubles, so that we can comfort those in any trouble with the comfort we ourselves have received from God."

It seemed that this principle of His truly worked out in Miz Mac's life. The traumatic and awful experiences associated with the untimely death of her beloved husband strengthened, taught, and enabled her to minister to others in similar situations throughout her lifetime. She never lacked opportunities.

"A few years after the Young boy died, Mr. Bill Moore, who had been such a good neighbor through all the years, died with cancer. We had to take care of him, too. Stanley went to a telephone about 18 miles away and called the Doctor and ambulance from Clayton.

Another incident involved Miz Mac's close friends, the Chilcote's.

"Mr. and Mrs. Chilcote were my neighbors for 17 years, and we exchanged work all that time. I had a good binder and feed rack so Mr. Chilcote would shock feed for me. In exchange, I'd bring the binder over to his place and cut his feed. In the fall, Mrs. Chilcote would come with him and fix dinner for us while we stacked feed together.

"Then, after the children were grown and Stanley and Marjorie were living on the ranch with me, Mr. Chilcote fell dead while feeding the chickens after working all day. So, they called on us again. We got him into the house. Then Stanley had to go 10 miles to call his son and the ambulance, while I got him all ready to go.

"Since the kids were on my place, I just moved over and stayed with Mrs. Chilcote and received 80 head of calves her husband had contracted for before his unexpected death. I had to wean, vaccinate, brand and feed them. We did the branding on Saturday's so Stanley could help. I stayed with Mrs. Chilcote until spring, and they found a man to work, Mr. Bobbitt. I countinued to exchange work with him for several years."

In addition to laying out the dead, Bernice was experienced with birthing. She even had the joy of helping deliver one of her own grandchildren, as her Grandmother Walsh had delivered her in Canada.

"Stanley and Marjorie were living on the ranch with me," Bernice remembered. "Stanley was working out, and we already had little Beulah. Two years later Reba was on the way. Marjorie planned to go to Clayton to the hospital in a few days, and we thought all was well but at two one morning she got real sick. When Stanley came to tell me I found out it was too late to start to town with her. I sent Stanley for a neighbor lady, Mrs. Moore, and just as they got back an hour later, Reba arrived. No doctor again, but we got over it OK.

"We didn't have a phone, so Stanley drove the school bus into Clayton for the Doctor. It was raining and they had some trouble geting back. It was about 6 pm when they finally arrived, but Dr. Landis said everything was all right. It was quite a relief for us to know for sure, though. The doctor spent the night and Stanley took him home as he took the children to school on the bus the next morning."

Probably as often as she was called on to stand in for a medical doctor (even to the extent of setting broken bones), Miz Mac was called on for veterinary services. That was something she enjoyed.

"I have done a lot of veterinary work over the long years. I only called a vet two times for my own needs. I always did Mr. Chilcote's vet work and was called on by other neighbors as well. I had real good luck, and rather liked the job. For a lot of years I guess I was the only vet they had out in our country. I delivered horses, and remember showing Rex Reeves how to deliver a colt once. It all goes with pioneer life, and I wish I could do it over again.

"You know, burnt alum is a wonderful medicine. You just put lump alum on a hot skillet on the stove and boil all the moisture out of it. It will form a hard crust as it cools. Then you pound it to powder and you've got the cure for lots of things. I never had a wirecut sewn up on a horse. Burnt alum will eat out proud flesh in that kind of sores. I've taken sores out of cows eyes by using it, too."

Even at 87, Miz Mac was was still a practicing vet. Her last and favorite horse, Taffy, sustained a wirecut while she was gone to Canada on a visit.

She later wrote in a letter, "Taffy got cut in the wire, just a front foot. I have it doing real good, but it will leave a scar. She never has been lame after the first week, but it sure has been quite a long seige of working with it."

In a 1989 letter addressed to Miz Mac's daughter Wanda, Mrs. Murray Dodson (who was Miz Mac's neighbor in 1949 & '50) said, "Mrs. Mac made a lasting impression on me. I remember spending the night with her and Stanley came to the door and told her he had hung a deer in the shed for her. Next morning she handed me a long-bladed knife and said, 'Let's go skin that deer.' I had never skinned anything in my life, but I tried . . ."

Miz Mac once said, "A Spanish guy taught me to skin a sheep. Beulah had a sheep that would run away. It ran clear to Seneca, so I just butchered and skinned it there. I waited a while for Stanley, but finally did it myself."

Other skills of Miz Mac's were helpful in the community. "I've sewed shoes [*put on half-soles*] for everybody in the country," she'd laugh, "and cut hair, too."

In addition to this kind of individual helpfulness, Miz Mac had a wonderful ability of leadership and organization. These qualities were put to work for the benefit of her neighbors in several different ways.

The rural neighbors are grateful for her untiring efforts on behalf of the road (now New Mexico State #370) which connects the McLaughlin Triple Link Ranch to Clayton, 25 miles away.

In 1971 Miz Mac said, "I have put in lots of time and miles trying to get a better road North from Clayton to the Colorado line. We have 12 miles of it paved so far, and all the bridges in as far out as 40 miles.

And we hope to get the North end connected to Colorado State High-way #71 at the state line before long. I am still working on this project and really enjoy it."

A paved highway on that route would greatly facilitate North/South travel through the region. It would avoid the Westward swing now necessary to cross the Colorado/New Mexico line over Raton Pass by allowing travel at the East end of that otherwise impassable mountain range. This would also, of course, funnel a good deal more traffic through Clayton, improving the economy there.

One major barrier to the improvement of the road North from Clayton was Corrumpa Creek, 25 miles North of town. The temper-amental, ever-changing stream often flooded in the Spring.

"Everybody said, 'You'll never get a bridge across that Corrumpa, what's the use of wasting your time?' ", Miz Mac recalled.

True to her reputation of doing the impossible, she kept harping at the highway engineers, insisting it was possible.

"They couldn't put a bridge in where the section lines crossed, but all they had to do was go upstream a ways and there was a rock as big as a house."

One of the problems was that unstable, shifting sand covered the bedrock to a depth of 90 feet along most of the Corrumpa, but it was found to be only 12 feet deep at the site Miz Mac selected. She even obtained right-of-way from the landowner, Ferol Smith.

Miz Mac always laughed to recall, "The engineers had me come down there and show them where to put the bridge. In a day or two, when they'd started driving piles, I stopped by. The head engineer was there and he said to me, 'I want to ask you a question. How come you to think about this location for the bridge?'

"I said, 'Well, seventh grade was as far as I went in school, but I can sit on the bank when the creek comes down and tell you where the bridge ought'a be. When you live in a country and watch things as long as I have, you learn something."

In addition to fighting for the bridge, Miz Mac collected some 900 signatures on a petition to improve Highway #370. In a belated gesture of admiration, some of the officials from whom she'd encountered the greatest resistance ordered a sign placed on the new bridge across Cor-rumpa Creek. The sign reads, "McLaughlin Bridge."

Miz Mac's neighbors in town as well as country benefitted from another job she tackled in 1970, at the age of 79. The only hospital in the town of 3500 had closed, due to the fact that one doctor had resigned and the other had retired due to ill health. It was 45 miles to

Dalhart, Texas, 135 miles to Amarillo, or 85 miles to Raton, New Mexico — the three closest places to receive any kind of medical attention. One man had died on the way to Amarillo, and families with small children as well as the elderly were in mass exodus from Clayton to areas where doctors were readily available. The entire community — schools, businessmen, and property owners, were being adversely affected.

An emergency meeting of civic groups was called, and Miz Mac was there, along with other members of her 20th Century Club. As a result of that meeting, the club promptly called a general meeting and formed a Civic Improvement Committee. Selected as Chairman of that committee, Miz Mac took two others and journeyed to Albuquerque for a workshop.

"This was a great help, because we learned how to make our efforts count better," she recalled. "We formed a Board of Directors, with the Jaycees agreeing to write and call doctors, seeking any who might be interested in coming to Clayton to practice. Our 20th Century club furnished womanpower and postage to write hundreds of letters."

It was soon discovered that all the doctors shared a common concern. They wanted a Medical Center to headquarter in and work from.

"Many people in town said it couldn't be done because we already had hospital bonds to pay off. Others said we didn't need a Medical Center, or that there were already vacant buildings in town that would be good enough. However, the people who were working so diligently and speaking personally with the doctors realized we'd never get doctors to practice here unless we had a modern facility to offer them," Bernice recalled.

"By that time we decided it was necessary to form a legal organization, so Clayton Medical Offices was organized and incorporated under state law, including some women on the Board. Shares went on sale to the general public, with $65,000 to be sold before a contract could be let for the building. Shares were offered in $25, $50, and $100 denominations so that anyone could help a little.

"Lots were obtained just across the street from the hospital, with the owner trading them for shares at a very reasonable price. Then our CIP committee asked the entire 20th Century Club to help sell shares. Some of the women canvassed the county and outlying areas with their own cars to sell shares. Others set up booths in the two banks and asked women from other civic groups to help sell there. We contacted everyone who came into the banks for several weeks, and we turned out be pretty good salesmen, seldom taking 'No' for an answer. The men canvassed the streets and business places and appealed to their own civic organizations.

"By this time the Farmers and Stockmens Bank saw that we 'meant business' so they stepped in with a matching offer, to buy a share for every share we sold elsewhere. They in turn donated their shares to worthwhile organizations, such as local churches.

"This gave us even more zeal and after the people saw what progress was being made everyone got behind the project. The community spirit was wonderful! Many people who had already bought some shares now **sacrificed** to buy more. As a result, the $65,000 goal was reached, the contract was let, and construction started.

"The Hospital was re-opened in August, 1971, and by September the Medical Offices building was completed, with room for three doctors sharing one reception room. Two doctors promptly moved in and a third promised to come soon. The entire community was very proud of the new facility and the part each one had in helping.

"The Jaycees put in the sidewalks and the Lions Club landscaped the grounds. Several people who had moved away returned, and the project has been a tool for building community loyalty and will continue to help us grow."

That statement was part of a report Miz Mac prepared in 1972, at the age of 91, rounding out her duties as Chariman of the Civic Improvement Committee. Still young at heart and active in mind and body, she continued to live up to her reputation as "the amazing Miz Mac."

At 87 she declared she could still fix a flat tire if she had one, and was not afraid to stay alone at the ranch.

"Nobody'd run off with me," she laughed, "and they'd bring me back soon as it got daylight if they did!"

Miz Mac, sister Mary and daughter Wanda at the McLaughlin Bridge across Corrumpa Creek.

11 Still Ranching

Miz Mac continued to be a rancher heart and soul, even after her children had grown and moved away to establish their own families. She always raised, broke and trained her own horses and mules with which to do the farming and riding associated with her operation.

One oft'told tale associated with her horse breeding is illustrative of both her tenacity and her quick thought. There was a stallion in the country with which she was very impressed, partly because he had a good, running walk. She wanted some colts sired by this horse, so approached his owner about bringing two of her mares.

The owner told her he'd taken in some outside mares the year before but it had proved considerable trouble and he'd decided to stand the horse only to his own mares.

Undaunted, Miz Mac said, "Well then, you'll just have to buy my two mares and sell them back to me this fall, safe in foal."

"You would think of some way," the owner laughed; and of course she got her colts from the running-walking stallion. Both fillies, she named them Silk and Satin and they were always favorites for riding as well as providing a sound foundation for a good line of saddle horses.

A filly called Rainbow, foaled by a good Thoroughbred mare of Miz Mac's, starred in a story of Old West intrigue.

Here's how she told the tale: "I'd always broke all my own horses, but Mrs. Chilcote just had a fit. She thought it was an awful thing and I shouldn't be doing it. So there was this kid workin' on the JE, and he'd ride by all the time going to get their mail. I could see he was a good hand, so I asked him about riding the filly and he said 'Sure,' he'd break her.

"I made him promise never to let her buck, because her mother had been a little bad that way and I didn't want her ever to get started. I'd

*Wanda and Stanley with
Rainbow and her foal, Ruby.*

seen him riding her after the mail a few times and she was going pretty nice. I was thinking I'd just as well go get her, when the boy got mixed up in a cow stealing deal.

"They were taking the stolen cattle over to those corrals East of the 7L Butte, across the Colorado line, and branding them. One day the law caught them and took all the cattle. He was riding my horse that day, and she just disappeared.

"I made several trips all over the country hunting her, but I could never turn her up. After a long time they had a trial and called me in for a character witness for the boy. I never did have to testify, but I visited with the Sheriff, Bob Dabney. I had a picture of that filly, showing some real distinctive little markings on one hind foot that would easily identify her. I gave it to the Sheriff and said, 'This is that mare I'm missing. Don't you lose this picture, because it's the only identification I have for her.'

"Some time later he called me and said he thought he'd found my filly, but I was going to have to go and get her. She was in a pasture belonging to an old man up by Kim, Colorado. She'd been there nearly a year and he wasn't about to give her up unless I could prove she was mine. I said that was alright with me, and got Earl to come over and stay with the kids so I could go. That was during the time we were milking all those cows.

"I took my old saddlehorse Dan, and left about three in the afternoon. I thought I'd never get to Likes; nearly didn't find the place in the dark. I'd been there a lot of times, around by the road, but this time I was going straight in, by Peacock Canyon. I finally did get there, and spent the night.

"Mrs. Like went with me to the bottom of the hill the next morning to show me how to get down a certain canyon. Then I went around, right by that corral where they'd branded those stolen cattle over from the 7L Butte, and on to the Dabney place. They gave me a fresh horse there, and the Dabney girl went with me. The old man's place where the filly was was only about five miles out of Kim.

"We got over there and he ran the horses in the corral and I said, 'Yes, that's her, in the back there, so wild she's staying clear against the fence.'

"You see, a bunch of young cowboys had been coming out there every weekend and roping her and saddling her up and using her for bronc riding practice. She'd gotten a kind of outlaw reputation because one guy was trying to catch her and he couldn't so he went to whip her with the bridle and she kicked him in the face. Knocked him out and left him for dead. So, she was ruined, from all that rodeoing.

"But the old man finally got her roped and then after a while I got up to her. She knew my voice and when I got my hands on her she began to calm down. I rubbed her around on the neck and shoulder a while, then worked on down her ribs and over her rump, and pulled on her tail a little. Then I went to the other side and did the same thing and she was relaxing quite a lot. But it just scared that old man to death. He knew about her kicking that guy and he told me never to do that again, that she'd kill me.

"Well, I got on my horse and led her home. Got back to the Dabney place that night and made it on home the third day after I'd started.

"Johnny Like was rodeoing then, and he heard I'd gotten the mare back, so he came by. I asked him, 'Johnny, will you take that mare and ride her a week and not let her buck?'

"He grinned and said he'd try, but he couldn't promise anything. But he did take her and ride her a week, and when he brought her back I rode her after the cows. I rode her a couple of times, but I could see the first time I did anything she didn't like she was going to buck me off, so I gave up. I just put the running W on her and broke her for a work horse.

"I used that running W a lot breaking horses and mules, and it would sure teach one what I meant when I said 'whoa!' This mare wasn't of a mind to pay any attention to me, so I just put the W on her and tied the end to a snubbin' post out in the corral. Then I let her loose and about the time she got to the end of the rope I hollered 'Whoa!' Well, she sure turned a somersault, but from then on when I'd just tighten up that line on the W she'd begin to whoa.

"I always used my voice a lot with horses, and my eyes. You can't tell me a horse can't read me just like I can read you, by the eyes!", Miz Mac would declare.

The year 1957 was a memorable one in the livestock business on the Triple Link. Miz Mac recalled, 'It was Thursday, the 20th of March. I had all my cows and 30 baby calves in the West pasture. I had company. Stanly and Reba, Loris' brother Earl, and Mr. Kendrick were all there. We fed that morning and then at 4:30 that afternoon it started snowing and blowing real bad.

"The storm continued through the night and all of Friday, in fact right on over the weekend and all day Sunday. We fed on Saturday, but it would have been best not to. A bunch of cows we weren't able to see in the blizzard came across a draw to where they had heard us, and their calves couldn't get through the drifts.

"By Monday morning the storm was lulling some, but the snow was real deep. We called the cattle all over home to feed hay, and the cows eyes were all covered with ice. I thought I had most of my calves, but by noon the ice was thawing off of them and I discovered that ten of the calves with my cows belonged to a neighbor. I only had five of my own.

"That left me short 25 calves, and we later discovered that when they'd gotten separated from the cows on Saturday they drifted South through a fence. We found them all dead, and that really hurt – losing 25 in one night! But I lived through it and just kept on going."

In 1971, when Bernice was 80, her children strongly urged her to get out of the cattle business and "Stop getting out in storms to feed," as

Miz Mac's horses, in 1958.
She loved baby colts.

The family grows up. Miz Mac stands between Stanley and Wanda on the first day of school in the fall of 1929.

she put it. She had a herd of 80 head at the time, and sold all but four nurse cows.

"I made them each raise four calves every year, though," Bernice said some time later. "It was a chore job, but I liked to do it. Then the children wanted me to sell them, so I did and just kept two 300# calves for beef."

Having her own beef was one of the last traditions Miz Mac clung to. Her father had been a butcher, and she'd never thought meat came from the market. Rather, it had been a product of her own hard work, usually from calving to table, and she always participated in the butchering.

Writing in December of 1981, following her 90th birthday, Miz Mac said, "I can still do pretty well at working. Wanda and I wrapped an 800 pound steer up in 5 hours on Friday. The men did the cutting, we the wrapping. They thought I should sit down but I said, 'That is no good for me.' I always stand up to do most things.

"We had the beef butchered up North of Des Moines and came by the ranch to leave half of it. Changing it to the deep freeze was the hardest part."

In 1978, Miz Mac was still staying at the ranch as much as possible, and wrote the following on February 8: "Right now we are having an ice storm with 5" of snow already on the ground. No mail today. The snow is 12" deep up at Des Moines. Wanda just called me and the phone is going out. As usual, when it comes a lot of moisture, it gets wet and quits. But don't worry about me.

"I have lots to eat and a 1,000 gallon tank of fuel, some coal oil for light if the lights go out, and lots of candles. Flour to make bread if

I have to, a big 22' freezer full of meat and vegetables as well as the pantry full of canned food. I try to always be prepared for the worst.

"In 1974 I got snowed in for two weeks. Then the grader opened up the road — it was wonderful. I went to Clayton to get some cake for my four cows and Wanda wanted me to stay all night. I had an idea I better get home, and the very next day it set in and snowed and blowed the roads all shut for one more week!"

When her family at last persuaded her to sell off most of her cattle, Miz Mac put her land into the soil bank. "That gave me more time to spend around the place," she said. "I have it all landscaped real nice, all my own planning, and I am enjoying it very much."

Miz Mac lived on the ranch until she was past ninety, sometimes spending part of the winter months at Wanda's home in Clayton. She continued to keep her dog, three cats and a special horse, Taffy. After the soil bank time was up, she leased her property to a neighbor, and always continued to take a big interest in the livestock running there, whether cows and calves or steers. Her letters always referred to the weather, the progress of the grass (and her thankfulness for rain) in summer, and the severity of the storms (and her concern for the livestock) in winter. The habits of a lifetime are not easily broken.

Her love of animals was one such habit. During the last year of her life, Miz Mac told a friend, "I never met an animal that didn't like me except one little coyote that I kept for a man. I told him I didn't like coyotes, but I'd keep it for him.

"Of course I'd killed coyotes for years and I just hated them. That little one must have known it. He wouldn't eat when I was around. I'd leave the food and go away, and when I'd come back the food would be gone. But the pup never would eat in front of me.

"When I'd go out there, that little coyote would look at me with something terrible in its eyes. But when Reba, my granddaughter was with me, the pup's whole countenance changed. You could just see love in it.

"When the man left it for me to care for, he tied it to a tree limb from overhead. I asked him if he wasn't afraid it would climb the tree and hang itself, but he told me coyotes won't climb. But, the day before the owner returned that crazy thing climbed the tree, jumped out, and killed himself."

Birthdays were special occasions for Miz Mac as the decades stacked up. In 1971 she wrote, "The children had a birthday party for me when I was 80 years old. There were around 140 people here from Colorado, Oklahoma, Texas and New Mexico. Relatives also came from Canada and Colorado. The party was a great success and I really did appreciate so many friends and old neighbors. It didn't even make me tired, and I'm so thankful for all of it. I am just not going to quit being active for many years yet, I hope. I feel that work and the great outdoors is the secret of health and happiness for me."

Speaking of health secrets, one of Miz Mac's was a daily nap. "I always took a nap. Everybody ought to do it," she'd laugh. "Right after dinner, I'd make the kids go outside. Ten minutes is all you really need, and then I'd be right back out in the field."

One of the amazing Miz Mac's secrets of happiness was caring for others. After her 80th birthday she wrote, "I always have a big supply of canned food and lots of fruit. The last few years I've had raspberries, strawberries, grapes and plums besides my peaches, apples, cherries and pears. I enjoy giving a Christmas package of jam and jelly to the old people [*note this*] who used to can and are not able any more. I also divide with the children."

The summer Bernice was 89 her 9 big peach trees bore a bumper crop. She said, "The peaches were the best I ever have seen in new Mexico. We filled all our jars, froze all we had room for and gave away all that our folks and friends would use. Wanda and I canned peaches, pickles, tomatoes and okra."

Because she loved to raise and can produce of all kinds, one of the rooms she included in the expansion of her ranch house was a pantry.

Bernice also always loved to cook, and to entertain and have her family together. In late 1979 she wrote, "I have my bid in for New Year's dinner this time. I cook the turkey and cranberries and the coffee and the girls bring the extras so it's not much work for any of us."

At Christmas in 1981 she wrote, "I had all the family together for Thanksgiving at the ranch this year. The next day Wanda and Stanley gave me a big birthday party at the church. There again I had my two children, four grandchildren, six great-grandchildren and two great-great grandchildren. So many people helped make it a wonderful day with lovely cards, flowers, telegrams, money and gifts. I love them all, God bless each one! I surely am thankful to God for my 90 years of good health and good family and friends."

Throughout her life, Miz Mac always had pet cats. This is Boots.

12   Honors

Over the years the many and varied accomplishments of the amazing Miz Mac were acknowledged by several noteworthy honors.

First was her 1953 designation as a Banker's Award Winner of the Northeastern Soil Conservation District of New Mexico. A news item announcing the award said, "Mrs. McLaughlin has operated her present ranch approximately 37 years. Her range land is in a high state of production, which shows that she has done a good job of grass management. She has developed adequate stock water and terraced her cropland to prevent water erosion."

Miz Mac was the first, and as far as we can determine the only, New Mexico woman to be honored with this type of soil conservation award.

In 1959 she was nominated for consideration as a top homemaker. The competition, sponsored by Western Farm Life, was for Top Homemaker in Union County. Miz Mac represented the Yucca club (of which she was a charter member), and the county contest judges chose her over the other twelve entries. The next step was district competition in July, where she represented Union County against the top homemakers of Curry, Colfax, Guadalupe, Harding, Quay, San Miguel and Mora Counties.

From that group she was chosen Top District Homemaker, which propelled her directly into State competition. Miz Mac had been to Canada on one of her frequent visits and when she arrived home there was ranch work to be caught up. Thus it happened that when the state judges for Top Homemaker arrived, they found their contestant not in the kitchen, or even in the garden, but rather in the corral, quite bloody—in the midst of dehorning a bunch of heifers!

After years Miz Mac's cheeks would still grow pink recalling her chagrin at facing those judges in that situation. However, it evidently did not hurt her image in their eyes. She asked them to allow her 30 minutes to clean up, and then entertained them in her usual hospitable fashion.

After visiting all the district winners across New Mexico's "Land of Enchantment," they chose Bernice McLaughlin as Top New Mexico Homemaker of 1959.

"I didn't really feel entitled to it," the modest lady said. "I went down to Albuquerque for the presentation. The prize was $100 to buy a new wardrobe, but I had to look for two days to find any clothes I'd have!"

Bernice was loved by her peers and in the course of years was elected to serve as President of both the Yucca Extension Club and the 20th Century Club. In 1963 she was named "Artist of the Year" for the Art Division of the 20th Century Club.

Although she never tried her hand as an artist until in her seventies the years hadn't dimmed the obvious talent her first schoolteacher in Canada had recognized. Miz Mac became proficient with watercolors, pastels and oils, and won many prizes for her artwork. She remained active in the art club into her nineties.

One year the 20th Century Club of Clayton took 18 items to the District Three convention of the New Mexico Federation of Women's Clubs at Portales, and won 17 ribbons. Miz Mac, then in her eighties, accounted for two of those ribbons—first with a pastel and third with a needlepoint.

Miz Mac was proficient in all the needlecrafts, including embroidery, crochet, and knitting. Over the years she accumulated a shoebox

A 1950 photo of the Yucca Club, of which Miz Mac was a Charter Member. Left to right, Miz Mac, Viola Long, Mattie Behm, Mrs. Everett, Ruth Belew, Lola Geary, Hazel Peet, Clara Irons, unknown, Marie Weiland and Louise Long.

Wearing the new outfit she won as Top New Mexico Homemaker.

full of fair ribbons won on her handiwork and her home canned produce.

Probably her proudest honor was induction into the National Cowgirl Hall of Fame and Western Heritage Center in Hereford, Texas in 1977 as a Western Heritage honoree.

Charles Arnett, a favorite friend of Miz Mac's, thought of her while reading a news item about the National Cowgirl Hall of Fame and their search for deserving nominees. He brought it to the attention of her daughter.

"Charles said, 'Your mother should be in there, if anybody should,' Wanda recalled. So I nominated her and submitted the information they requested."

Miz Mac was chosen by a careful and well-qualified Hall of Fame Selection Committee from among 250 nominees. She was honored by induction to the National Cowgirl Hall of Fame & Western Heritage

With friend Marie Stringer at the unveiling of her portrait during Cowgirl Hall of Fame ceremonies, 1984.

Center because of her pioneering efforts in two nations. They recognized her enterprise, fortitude and ability as a successful ranchwoman, along with her embodiment of the true pioneer spirit of Western women.

In her Christmas letter of 1977 Miz Mac wrote: "I had a very nice honor in May this year. I was chosen to be inducted into the National Cowgirl Hall of Fame in Hereford, Texas. The professional All Girl rodeo was held in conjunction with the other ceremonies and was a lovely affair all one day; starting with a breakfast, then parade, luncheon, art show and organ concert in the afternoon; the rodeo that evening with the induction ceremonies in the rodeo arena, then a reception after the rodeo. It was a big day and all my family and lots of friends attended the festivities and helped to make my day again. I received a lovely engraved bronze plaque and many other gifts."

With her quick wit, lovable nature, and kindly ways, Miz Mac became an instant favorite at the Hall of Fame, and she was nearly always in attendance for the annual honoree induction ceremonies there from 1977 until the time of her death.

She was selected as "cover girl" for the NCHOF's annual publication, Sidesaddle, in 1984. Her portrait was done by Harvey Gary Hammett of Hereford, Texas, and she was on hand for the unveiling. The artist presented the large original to the Hall of Fame for its permanent collection, and it hangs there today.

A tree planted in Miz Mac's memory now grows in the Hall of Fame memorial garden, and a collection of her Western memorabilia is on display there.

Miz Mac has also been honored at Heritage Park in Calgary, Alberta, Canada. The story of her early life is in the Archives there, and her picture also hangs there.

Miz Mac at the National Cowgirl Hall of Fame the day of her induction, 1977.

The amazing Miz Mac when she was chosen Top New Mexico Homemaker. In front of the fireplace in her homestead house.

13 The Canadian Connection

The Walsh family was large, and very close. Through the years when sister Bernie struggled to rear her children alone and carve a ranch from the New Mexico prairie, her Canadian siblings took turns coming to the states to be with her for extended periods of time.

When things became easier for her and she had time to travel, she was extremely fond of returning to Canada to visit them, and made it almost an annual tradition. As late as the mid 1970's her brother Harold was still living in the log home where Bernie was born, so of course she always returned to the homestead. And, if she didn't go to Canada, she wanted some of the family to come down and visit her. The land is still in the family, owned now by Bernie's nephew, Loris Walsh.

Being in Canada during the Calgary Stampede and getting to see the rodeo and races was another love of Miz Mac's. She had ridden in the original Calgary Stampede rodeo parade in 1912, and was invited to attend the Golden Anniversary event in 1962.

"They wanted to know if I'd like to ride in a wagon or in a car," she snorted indignantly, "and I told 'em I'd ride a horse, just like I did the first time!"

In 1940 Bernie's brother, Harley Walsh, won the North American Saddle Bronc Riding Championship, as well as the Canadian Saddle Bronc Riding Championship. Bernie and her children were in Calgary to watch his winning rides and cheer him on.

Bernie's daughter, Wanda Hughes said, "During the hard years of drought, dustbowl and depression, our family in Canada encouraged us through letters, and several of them came to visit us. Aunt Mary was in the mission field in Peace River (Northern Alberta) and she was always faithful to write and assure us she was praying for us.

Harold Walsh on Sugar Beet at the Calgary Stampede.

"Mother had not been home nor seen her mother in 20 years. I was working in the Courthouse and was able to help financially, so I encouraged her to go to Canada. She went on the train and stayed about a month. It was a real treat for her, and after that she returned numerous times.

"She always talked about the Peace River country, where she and Daddy had planned to homestead. She wanted to see it, so when I retired in 1979 we made the trip. We picked up Aunt Mary in Denver and Aunt Martha in Calgary, and drove to the beautiful Peace River Valley. It was a special treat for all of us."

In July of 1977, when she was 85, Miz Mac went to North Carolina to visit her brother Harold and his wife Enid. She wrote afterward, "We rode horseback nearly every day for two weeks. I sure did enjoy riding with them, but not the [*fox*] hunting. Then Harold and his wife both got sick, so I stayed another two weeks. I just might have to go back later, so I can't plan on going to Canada this year."

Later that year Harley visited Bernie for two weeks on the ranch, but had to return home because of his wife's fatal illness.

"The first of December in 1977 Bernice wrote, 'I do hope to get to go to Canada next summer at Calgary Stampede time. I am feeling just great, but busy. I am expecting a second cousin by marriage from Yorkshire, England for Christmas. . .We have corresponded over the years but she has never been out of England."

A few weeks later the report was, "Louie Hustler from England came for Christmas, and Mary, my sister. Mary stayed a week, Louie three weeks, and we surely did have a wonderful visit. Now I would like to go to England!

"The weather was real nice all the time Louie was here, just a little cold and windy one day. We got to see most of the country and quite a lot of my friends. . .Took in art club, Louie had never tried painting but we each painted a little wood oval plaque with strawberries and they are real cute. We only got in [*to Clayton*] one time to Art Club, so we had to finish at home."

The summer of 1978 Bernie returned to Canada for three weeks of visiting. She said, "We had a reunion, 8 of us, between the ages of 74 and 88."

In February of 1980 Bernie wrote, "My younger sister Martha came down three weeks ago to Denver and visited with my sister Mary for a couple of weeks, then came on down here the first of last week. We stayed in Clayton with Wanda until Tuesday, then came out to the ranch. It got to 4 degrees above here, but very little snow and no wind, now today the sun has been shining beautifully all day.

"I'm looking forward to the spring weather, I don't like wintertime like I used to. I have been feeling real good all winter, no aches or pains so far, just a bit of a cold. Surely am thankful for my good health."

In late March, 1981, Miz Mac wrote, "I had my 89th birthday with Wanda's boys in Albuquerque. It was on Thanksgiving Day this year, so we really did have a good day. I've stayed in Clayton at Wanda's a lot this winter. Got out to the ranch about two or three times a week and have stayed three days at a time when the weather and the roads were OK.

*Haying on the home
place in Canada.*

Harley Walsh on Smallpox at the Calgary Stampede.

Harley Walsh on Grandma at the Calgary Stampede.

"I still enjoy my driving. I had my eyes checked last week and the eye man said 'You have extra good eyes yet, don't worry about having to give up driving.' I don't go home after night anymore, but get home before sundown. I have not had a cold all winter, so that is something to be thankful for.

"I sure do hope to get back up to Alberta this summer, but haven't got it all planned out yet. My youngest brother died up there a month ago, but it was real bad weather here and I just didn't try to go."

In her 1981 Christmas letter, Miz Mac wrote, "I left right after the 4th of July for Canada. Took the bus to Castle Rock, Colorado, and our good friend Sybil met me there. I spent several hours with her, then she put me on the plane in Denver. I was in Calgary in two hours, where Dick and Clara met me and I spent several days with sister Martha.

"Then went out to the old homestead where I was born, and visited the rest of the family and friends near Madden for over a month. Sister Mary was there also, and I went back to Abbotsford, British Columbia, with her. I spent about two weeks with Mary, sister Grace and niece Bernice. We went to Vancouver to visit other relatives, then took the big ferry to Victoria to visit sister Elsie. I flew back to Denver from Vancouver, and spent two days with friends before coming on home. I surely did enjoy it all."

In another letter in December of 1981, Miz Mac added, "While I was in Calgary we all came down to Bozeman, Montana to visit the girl that makes those bronzes. [*Pamela Harr, noted Western sculptor whom Miz Mac had met at the National Cowgirl Hall of Fame & Western Heritage Center.*] You should see that outfit. It was 300 miles down there from Calgary.

"I have a friend living there who used to work for my dad when I was a teenager. My nephew Dick Havens had promised them that if Mary, Martha and I ever got out there together he was going to bring us down, and nothing else would do. It was a nice trip and we sure had a real good time, four days. It took almost a day each way, but we saw a lot of pretty country."

A Walsh family reunion. Left to right, Bernie, brother Hiriam and his wife Flo, Bernie's parents Laura and Richard Walsh, sister Mary, brother-in-law Ray Havens and sister Martha Havens, sister-in-law Dorothy and brother Angus Walsh. In front, seated, nephews Loris Walsh and Richard Havens.

14   Through the Eyes of Her Friends

The friends Miz Mac made in her 93 years are uncountable. Many of them were especially close, and have fond recollections of instances which portray her inimitable character and the multiple and varied facets of her personality.

Hugh Cozart of Cove, Colorado, wrote, "My first memory of Mama Mac is associated with some wonderful fresh peaches she brought to a picnic. My father, Cy Cozart, and Mama Mac's son Stanley both worked for Colorado Interstate Gas, and a group of us gathered at Fisher's Peak north of Raton, NM, for this picnic.

"I recall the peaches as being very big, juicy and delicious, and everyone was raving about them. It seems that years earlier Mama Mac had bought some peaches, and later took the time and trouble to plant the pits in a wet spot down near her windmill, so she had peach trees – in Northern New Mexico!

"When I was around 15 years of age, I worked for Mama Mac one full summer, and at other odd times when I could.

"Her house was built flush with the ground and the lawn ran clear up to the door. Mama Mac decided she wanted to go to a rocky, dry wash for a big – really big – flat rock to put in front of the door.

"One day she reported that, while out riding, she had found 'just the rock.' She gathered the best manpower she could find that day, which consisted of me, a willing but slight teenager, and Mr. Kendrick, who was 80 and no doubt past his prime!

"She drove us there in the pickup. She backed into a bank so that the slab she'd chosen could be moved forward and lowered into the truck. The rust-colored rock she'd picked was about three feet wide and six feet long and two to three inches thick.

"We loosened the rock and moved it forward by rolling it over small pieces of pipe. Unloading it in front of the door involved much the same process. We spent from seven in the morning until probably four in the afternoon—all day—at the task.

"I later helped this resourceful lady build a garage of surplus munitions boxes after World War II. Once again, it was Mr. Kendrick, Mama Mac and me. The boxes were about 16" x 12" x 12". They had lids, which we nailed shut to make them stronger.

"I believe we poured a concrete footer, then began stacking the boxes, staggering the joints and toe-nailing each box in place. Rafters and roofing were all it took to finish it off. Then the sides were stuccoed. The resulting garage was about 24 foot square.

"On any Sunday you'd likely find a bunch of us high school kids at Mama Mac's. It was usually her granddaughters Reba and Beulah, Billy Hittson, my brother Wayne and me. Mama Mac would always have a bull or a dry cow to bring in for us cowboys to try to ride.

"The WPA came to Mama Mac's country with roads and bridges to build. They hired local men with teams of horses to help move dirt. Mama Mac always had a fine team, and I remember her complaining that they wouldn't hire her and her team, simply because she was a woman.

"Each of these stories tells something of the character of Mama Mac.

"The rock stoop? Her 'all things possible' attitude and her creativity. She found a natural rock much more interesting than poured concrete.

"The peaches? Again, 'all things possible,' even to peaches in New Mexico; and her willingness to share.

"The garage? A thinking and creative mind.

"Letting kids ride her livestock? Mama Mac liked to have fun, and liked it best when stock was involved.

"The WPA? Was Mama Mac an early Equal Rights person?"

Friend Virginia Wagner of Clayton recalled Miz Mac as a disciplinarian and dispenser of "home remedies."

Virginia said, "To correct a difficult, bullheaded child she told me what to do. 'Just get ahold of the child and shake them until their teeth rattle.' No more trouble with them! To potty train a child was no challenge for Mrs. Mac. She had a very stern way of persuading them to sit or stand with a stool placed correctly in position until the job was accomplished. No problem! All people respected Mrs. Mac's authoritative ways.

"Mrs. Mac's remedy for a deep cough: '1/2 cup whiskey, 1/2 cup honey, 7 1/2 tablespoons glycerine, 1 1/2 teaspoons menthol crystals. Dissolve menthol crystals in whiskey; add other ingredients. Very good for cough.'

"Mrs. Mac fixed some for me—just one dose was enough for a complete cure. Another of her favorite remedies was a horse lineament called 'Beagle Oil.'

" 'No fooling,' Mrs. Mac would say. 'It is good for man or beast.' It was, good for animals or people, for whatever ailed them. She recommended it to one of her friends that I took care of for a short time. The lady would ask me to rub the Beagle Oil all over her, and it worked.

"Another salve that Mrs. Mac said every household shouldn't do without was 'Corona Hoof & Udder Balm.' You have guessed it—good for horses, cows, sheep, goats and people. All different types of ailments were cured with it.

"When I visited at Miz Mac's ranch once she explained how they built her beautiful fireplace. Mr. Kendrick built the form and Miz Mac placed the pieces of petrified wood just the way she wanted them, to create a pattern. She had carried the rock in from Corrumpa Creek, West of her ranch, and the fireplace is a lovely piece of art.

"All you had to say was 'rodeo' and Miz Mac was ready to go. I had the privilege to watch the National Finals on TV with her. She sat in my 'little girl' rocking chair very close to the TV so she could see it all. It was more interesting to watch Miz Mac watching the rodeo than to see the rodeo itself!

"The National Finals Steer Roping contest was held in Clayton once. The weather was so windy, rainy, sleet and cold that people didn't expect it to continue, but the ropers were all here so they had to go ahead with it. Miz Mac put on all the clothes she could find, including her wool hat, and was right there to watch.

"She had a lot of cute hats and caps that were just a part of her. She told me if you could keep your head covered, you'd be warm all over because you lost body heat out the top of your head. She said, 'anybody ought to know that.' In committee meetings that seemed to never end I've seen her take the soft crocheted cap off her head and place it in her chair for a cushion.

"She was one of my very favorite friends and I'm so happy I had the privilege of knowing her. Many pages could be written about her, but her love and friendship for me covers everything. Someone once said, 'Wisdom is knowing what to do; Skill is knowing how to do it; Virtue is doing it well.' Miz Mac had all three."

Lawson Long was a longtime neighbor of Miz Mac's. "We came to this country in 1911," he said. "The McLaughlin place was just 1/2 mile North and a mile East of where we lived, and 2 miles East of my old home place. It's a good country you know. We don't have any smog, but on the other hand you may never get rich here.

"Miz Mac was a real good neighbor. We worked together a lot. She was out and goin' most of the time, as long as she lived."

Lawson Long was one of the last people to see Loris McLaughlin alive, having visited with him in the field the afternoon he was killed.

Nikki A. Sharp of Clayton recalls, "Miz Mac was a very favorite person in my life. She always seemed to like me, and shared with me lots of thoughts and things she thought of as private.

"When I first moved to Clayton, my father-in-law told me about her. To illustrate her ability and versatility, he quoted a common saying in the community: 'The only thing Miz Mac can't do as well as a man is water a fence post!'

"The day before entering the hospital in her final illness, Miz Mac worked in her yard at the ranch, pulling dandelions and picking cherries. She once told me she didn't want to live if she couldn't work, and she always thanked the Lord in her prayers for the ability to work.

"The day before she died, I went to the hospital to visit her. Her daughter-in-law Marjorie and one other visitor were already there. Marjorie told me she didn't think Miz Mac had known they were there all afternoon, and she probably wouldn't know I was there, either. Miz Mac was lying on her back, very still, eyes closed. As the other visitor started telling Marjorie goodbye, I touched Miz Mac's arm, preparing also to leave.

"Much to my surprise she grabbed my hand, at the same time hushing me with a whispered, 'Shhh!'. When the other visitor was well out of the room she looked up at me and said, 'Oh, I thought that little old woman would never leave!'. I have laughed about that many times.

"Miz Mac was the kind of person I would hope I could be. I hope, also, that her memory will live on in the hearts of people for a long time to come, even when all of us are gone. She was indeed the symbol of the American dream and the fulfillment of womanhood."

A.D. Weatherly, who owns a large ranch near Des Moines, New Mexico, said, "We knew Miz Mac for over 40 years and remember her as a hardy, rugged individual who met all challenges head on. I can remember how she and my mother, Maggie Weatherly, would sit together at the Annual Cowboy Camp Meetings at Weatherly Grove and reminisce about the early pioneer days.

"When Miz Mac was up in her 70's she saw a young neighbor Milton Bennet's building which had been constructed from surplus ammunition boxes and said, 'I can do that!' And she did. She was an inspiration to the faint hearted during tough times."

Cluvarie (Mrs. Murray) Dodson lived neighbors to Miz Mac in 1949 and '50. She once wrote, "Mrs. Mac, as we affectionately called her, made a lasting impression on me. I have a snapshot of her with two granddaughters who sometimes came to our camp with her. I never ceased to be amazed at Mrs. Mac's ability, and in so many fields. While we were there she chased over those long, rough miles to Clayton to take art!"

Doyle Kear lived in Miz Mac's neighborhood and often leased her land after she retired. He recalls an incident after Miz Mac sold her beef herd but was raising calves on four nurse cows.

"She came home around 10 pm and got one of the nurse cows in the barn, fastening her head in the stanchion. While Miz Mac was gone to get the feed, the cow nosed into the separator bowl which served as a feed pan, disturbing a napping rattlesnake which was coiled up in there.

"The snake repeatedly struck the cow around the nose, since she was locked in the stanchion and with all the confusion and the weight of the cow pulling back it was a while before Miz Mac couldn't get the stanchion unlatched. She then ran to the house and phoned me. By the time I drove the few miles over there, she had fashioned a paddle with nails to pierce the skin and drain the poison out of the snakebites.

"We killed the snake, and although the cow's head was quite swollen and her breathing was labored we drained the wounds with the paddle and used snakebite medicine on her, and she lived to raise a lot more calves.

"In the years I leased the Triple Link and associated with Miz Mac, she taught me some very valuable lessons about the ranching business."

Lola (Mrs. J.C.) Geary, now of Dumas, Texas, was a longtime neighbor of Miz Mac's, living about five miles away. They shared many experiences and had a very close and loving relationship.

Lola recalled, "Miz Mac was interested in many things — church, nature, gardening, art, horses and cattle, all animals, neighbors and accomplishments. She loved to make things.

"She was much older than I, but when it came to working and many things, you'd have had to get a birth certificate to tell it. She could always do more work in a day than I could in a week.

"She always found a way, and did what had to be done, without complaint. One winter around 1945 Miz Mac pastured her cattle South of us about 4 or 5 miles. The snow was so deep vehicles couldn't move. Miz Mac would come to our house on horseback each evening and spend the night. Early the next morning she and J.C. would each take a sack of cake from our cake house and ride down and feed the cattle. Then she would ride home and take care of the rest of her day's work. This lasted quite a long time and we were lucky to have a good supply of cake laid in.

"About 1949 or 50 we had a terrible blizzard. A man up by Grenville was frozen to death. One of our neighbors became quite ill with pneumonia, and the roads had been closed for several days. Our rural phone line was working, so we got word to the highway department. They came and broke the road open and got him to the hospital.

"A few days later the weather had settled some, the sun was shining brightly, and everyone took advantage of the open road to go to town for supplies. My husband and son and I took the wife and three children of our sick neighbor into Clayton to visit him. We hadn't been there long when the wind started blowing real hard. We knew the plowed road would soon blow in, and we needed to get home to take care of our stock. There was no time to eat but everyone was hungry so we ran into a store and got lunchmeat and crackers; whatever we could find to eat on the road.

"The high winds whipped up a terrible ground blizzard, filling in the road very fast. Miz Mac was also in town, so she followed behind us with her car. Eight or ten miles out we couldn't see anything and the road was drifting in so fast we decided to turn around and go back.

"But, by then both cars were hopelessly stuck, and the road was drifted in behind us as badly as it was in front, so there we were. I immediately got sick from being so frightened that we'd all freeze to death. Miz Mac and my husband were out in that storm, shoveling snow. Clara, the neighbors wife, would periodically get out to relieve Miz Mac, but it was an impossible task because the wind was moving more snow than the shovels.

"I was nearly hysterical, and of course Miz Mac was as calm as always. My husband assured me we wouldn't freeze. He said we would walk to an abandoned house not too far off the road and burn the floor if nothing else to keep warm. All the kids were very calm, of course it was an adventure for them.

"Miz Mac got into our car, making eight of us, and we spent the night there in the snowdrifts. We ran the heater until the car ran out of gas sometime in the early morning. All we had was one small blanket and I made a vow to carry blankets, no matter what, from then on. With her usual alert foresight, Miz Mac wouldn't allow the window to be completely closed, for fear of asphyxiation from the exhaust fumes. We all got quite cold but had no frostbites.

"At daylight J.C. and Cliff, the oldest boy who was with us, set out to walk about 5 miles to the closest neighbor's to get a tractor and some gas and water. Miz Mac just would go with them, and couldn't be deterred. The snow was very deep, hard crusted on top yet not solid enough to support a person, so it was very hard walking, but she made it. My husband said she nearly collapsed at the door, and she did stay there while they brought the tractor back and got our car out. By then a pickup with two men had come out from town also, so they had more help. Miz Mac left her car right there for several days.

"Once when J.C. was gone, I saw a heifer having trouble calving. I always thought of Miz Mac whenever I needed help, so I went and got her immediately. The heifer was already in the corral. I was always afraid of stock, very clumsy and scared and almost useless. The heifer got on the fight and would take us every time we tried to drive her into the chute. I spent most of the time on the fence and was only a hindrance because Miz Mac was doubled up with laughter from watching me. She finally got the heifer where she wanted her, and I came down off my safe perch to help. She saved both the calf and heifer but each time she told the story she'd laugh so hard she almost cried to think of her good help! She always said she wished she had a movie of 'that episode.'

"Some years later we were living in Clayton. Miz Mac would occasionally come and spend a night with us. Whenever she visited we'd have a laughing spell over various funny things we'd recall from the past, giggling like schoolgirls. One time, we'd had our laugh and gone to bed and had been asleep for some time when Miz Mac came in and whispered that she had to go home, and had to go 'right now.'

"We inquired why and she said, 'I don't remember turning a burner off under something I had cooking on the stove.'

"It was a very cold night and there was snow on the ground but she quickly dressed and left. I didn't expect to see her until the next day or something, but later toward morning she slipped back in and got in bed. She warned us, 'Don't you ever tell Wanda about me doing that!'

"We went to Raton every summer to race horses. One summer I came out to spend a few days with Miz Mac. Our garage on the ranch had two wide doors and the loose horses got to backing up in there to get in the shade and out of the wind. They were pushing against the doors and about to push them in.

"When I left Raton, J.C. told me, 'While you're down there, hire somebody to come out from town and nail some boards up across those garage doors, before the horses ruin them.'

"Right after I got to Miz Mac's I asked her who she thought we could hire to come out and do the job. Her reply was, 'Oh, we can do that ourselves.'

"I protested that we didn't have any tools, any boards, or anything, and it was so terribly hot, so we should just get somebody. But all my talk was to no avail. We got over there about 9 am, and it was so hot. There were some old boards down behind the barn. Weeds had grown up all around them and some old gourd vines had twined around them and I just knew there were snakes everywhere. It was a terrible task and I was ready to quit before we started, but it wasn't any problem to Miz Mac, who said we'd get it done in 'nothing flat.'

"We eventually did and I was so tired and hot I thought I'd collapse, but she'd noticed some screens that were torn on the house windows, so we had to fix them, too, before we left. That took quite a little longer.

"Now, Miz Mac always napped after a meal, in fact she'd almost go to sleep in her plate, although she never napped for long. After the morning we'd put in, though, I thought surely we'd lie around the rest of the hot afternoon. I was exhausted.

"But Miz Mac had other plans. We cleaned out her garage that afternoon. I never worked so hard in my life. I couldn't give up and let her get ahead of me, although she always was. I had to try to keep up, which was always a task for me.

"Miz Mac was one of the first neighbors to welcome me to the community. Our love spanned a lot of years, right up until her death. I wish I could really relate the love and respect I had for this great lady. I loved her very much."

Howard Hughes spent a good deal of time at Miz Mac's through his growing up years, being the cousin of her grandsons. He shared some reminisces.

"I'm sure Miz Mac knew me when I was born, since I was born in that part of the country where she lived, but my first recollection of her was somewhere around 1942. My mother and I were down at Cuates due to sickness in the family. My great-grandfather ran the postoffice at Cuates.

"We were heading back into Clayton to catch the train home to Colorado Springs. For some reason my grandfather couldn't get away to take us in, so he hauled us over to Miz Macs because she was going to town anyway, I believe to sell milk. She had an old '39 or '40 Ford. Now, I've always liked Fords, and I sometimes think Miz Mac had something to do with that. Her old Ford smelled of milk — not soured milk, but fresh milk — a pleasant smell. And she gave us a ride to town.

"There were several creeks to cross, and it was a chore to get from Miz Mac's place to Clayton. She always knew where the crossings were, and although I recall my grandfather sometimes getting stuck in those creeks, I never remember Miz Mac getting stuck.

"Anytime we went to that area to visit, I went to see Miz Mac because I always had such a good time at her place. At all stages of my life, I seemed to learn quite a lot from her. She could teach you without seeming to teach, just by doing things. She'd do them slow enough you could catch on, and she'd show you how.

"I can never remember her being real cranky with me, although I never wanted to break anything or do anything bad at her place for fear she wouldn't want me to come back or wouldn't invite me back. My folks had taught me how to work when I was pretty young, and she always seemed glad to have me come. She'd feed me like I was starved, and then would just suggest that a fence needed to be fixed, or she had to work on a gate — she never ordered you out to do any work.

"I never remember her saying anything very 'catty' or vicious about anyone behind their back. If she didn't like something somebody was doing, she'd wait until they got there, and then she'd tell 'em to their face! I felt fortunate that she never told me I was a danged fool or anything, although a couple of times she suggested I might have used better judgement!

"I can remember her being upset with us boys, her grandson Loris and myself and a cousin of ours, when we rolled some big, heavy wagon wheels off a hill into a gully. She didn't lay a hand on us, or get real cranky with us, but we did have to push them 50 or 100 yards uphill to put them back where we found them.

"Another time she was really angry with Loris and I, the only time I ever remember her raising her voice at me. I never knew until I was fully grown just how badly we had frightened her.

"Her son Stanley had found a water tank, 12 or 15 feet high and mabye 10 feet across, with a steel top, a manhole in the top, and a ladder going down inside. This was going to be dismantled or junked, so they bought it and Miz Mac had a cement pad poured for it and fixed it so the overflow from her wooden water tank at the windmill would run into it. The water stored there was used for irrigating the garden and such.

"She had to go to town for something on a hot summer day, and Loris and I had some chores to do. Having finished those, we decided that big tank full of water would be a good place to cool off. We stripped off our clothes and climbed down the ladder and were havin' an awfully good time in the water when Miz Mac drove in, having forgotten something and returned to the ranch.

"Discovering us, she really got upset. I could swim and so could Loris, and there were two of us, so we weren't concerned. I didn't know until years later that Miz Mac couldn't swim and was deathly afraid of water. She told me she was scared to death we boys would drown in that water tank!

"I can recall that Miz Mac had electric lights very early. My grandfather didn't. She had a windcharger, and kept a bank of batteries upstairs. I remember her taking me up there and showing me those batteries and telling me that you didn't touch those, because they would burn your fingers.

"She had coal oil lights like my grandfather, but when we'd go to visit her she'd turn on that one lone electric light, hangin' from a wire down from the ceiling. It was hooked up to those batteries, and I was totally fascinated with it.

"Another thing I recall is that Miz Mac had a water faucet in her house, with a sink under it. My grandfather had a pitcher pump on the counter, but water would run from Miz Mac's faucet without pumping. She stored her water in the wooden tank, and the faucet was gravity-fed from there.

"Whenever I visited Miz Mac, she really fed me. She always insisted I eat a good breakfast. She liked getting the chores done early in the morning. Grandad would take Loris and I fishing, but there always seemed to be two or three cedar posts that needed to be peeled before we'd go. If there was any complaining, Miz Mac would let us know that they needed those posts, and the work had to be done.

"Her reprimanding was always done in a good way, to teach a lesson. She caught us boys swearing once. It was real hot weather and we were going barefoot and the rocks burned our feet I think, anyhow somebody said 'S.O.B.' and she overheard it. It was real funny the amount of chores that showed up about an hour later — enough to keep three boys very busy. Without being mean, she managed to find an awful lot of things that just had to be done right then.

"One of the humorous stories I recall hearing about Miz Mac regarded her art. She was an accomplished, self-taught artist. If anybody in the world knew what a windmill looked like, it was Miz Mac — but she was taking an art class and the subject to paint was a windmill. According to the story, she and this artist had a knock-down-drag-out verbal argument over the red rod. He claimed it didn't belong there, but she put it in anyhow. That painting still hangs in Wanda's home, and I have to agree with Miz Mac — it looks better with the red rod in it.

"She told me tales of breaking horses, using a broke team to break the green ones with. She traded work all around the area. I know there was a lot of jealousy, for the plain and simple reason that she had the gumption to get out and go to work. She was a soft lady in hard times, but could be as hard as she wanted to be.

"My great-grandfather, Mr. Kendrick, who had been her neighbor, sold his place and wandered somewhat aimlessly about for a few years after his wife died. He liked that area, and Miz Mac eventually took him on as a hired hand, when he was well over 60 years old. She boarded him and cared for him until he was up in his 80's, and although he still gardened and tried to do things, you know he didn't do a lot. I don't know if he was a burden or not, she never let on.

"She was very good to him, and probably promoted his longevity, since he did enjoy whiskey pretty well, but when Miz Mac was around he didn't get much of it. She definitely kept him from drinking as much as he would have. He did have bottles stashed in numerous hiding places around the ranch, though. Being kids, Loris and I knew where most of them were.

"Miz Mac always treated my wife and children like she'd known them all her life. One time we visited her after her vision had failed and all she had was peripheral vision. I hadn't seen her in five years, but when I knocked on the door at Wanda's and saw her get up to answer it I called to her, and she said 'Oh, Howard, I recognize your voice.' Makes a fell'a feel good to know that somebody remembers his voice, after all that time.

"Even the last time we saw her, when she was quite ill, her mind was very, very sharp and there was even some joking. I have never known a person who could instill so much confidence in another. I believe she had a lot to do with my growing up, even though I was a typical ornery kid. As she got older she was even freer to speak her mind than when she was younger, asking me things that I found rather amusing, concerning my life and what I'd done with it. She made the statement once that I should've stayed down there and worked with cows. Mabye she was right.

"I hope in my life I can be half the person she was. It was a real honor knowing and working with her."

W.C. Wheatley of Clayton, who served in the State Senate while Miz Mac was campaigning on her Highway 370 project, said, "The one word that described Miz Mac in her approach to life was persistence.

"For instance, I remember one time when Miz Mac came into my garage, the Clayton Automotive Service, to get some work done on her pickup. It was her chief transportation from the ranch since it would haul a large load of feed or salt and mabye some groceries she'd need in her lonesome living on the cow ranch she worked and maintained when she was many years older than most of her neighbors.

"This particular afternoon the sun was low in the Western horizon, making the East door of the garage pretty dark. Just inside I had installed a modern front-end alignment machine in a large pit. Miz Mac discovered this when her pickup ran into the machine.

"She got out, walked around behind her pickup and said to me, 'What did I do?'

"When the whole shop crew had finally managed to pull her pickup back onto the floor of the garage she said, 'You should have told me that hole was there! Now please get my pickup fixed so I can get on about my business.'

"She was hardly upset, and I think this illustrates the wonderful qualities of Miz Mac, who was a very personal friend of mine."

Lynn Hunsperger, whose family Bernie and Mary boarded with in Didsbury, Alberta, while attending the second grade, remembered her as 'a pioneer woman of great strength and perseverance.'

Hunsperger and his wife Joan, who still live at Didsbury, said, "Bernice McLaughlin was loved and known to many for her unusual accomplishments in spite of adversity. She loved to tell about her Calgary high jumping world record in 1911, and we recall delight her many visits in our home as Lynn and her exchanged 'horse stories.' A great lady, Bernie will always have a special place in our hearts."

Ray Banta of Crossfield, Alberta, said, "It's been 76 years since I first met Bernie, when she and her husband rented my father's ranch before they moved to 'the States.' Memories of a small lady full of energy and kindliness are still with me from that time.

"As years went by, word of her success as a ranch manager, under trying circumstances, and her prowess as a rider and stock person came back to this corner of Alberta. It was my pleasure to chat with Bernie at various times when she returned to visit relatives. Through all the years of her very active life, she never lost her delight in talking about her experiences as a young girl growing up in this part of Canada, where much depended on good horsemanship, something she excelled at."

Family friend Don Adams recalls the summer of 1947 when he went to work for Miz Mac on his 'first fulltime summer job.' He was 14-years-old.

Don recalls, "Stanley took me down to Miz Mac's late one day, the first part of June. I never dreamed that of all my summers, before and after, this would be the most remembered.

"The first day or two she showed and told me what my job would be — milking, taking care of horses, gardening, and plowing 160 acres of farmland. The second or third day I was so sunburned she decided I needed doctoring. She skimmed cream off the milk and rubbed it on my face. Anyone who knew Miz Mac would know what I went through, trying to keep from crying while she rubbed cream on my burned face with those hard, calloused hands that had done so much work.

"One day as we checked cattle she said, 'That cow with the cancer eye has to be taken care of tomorrow.' The next morning, after chores, we saddled up and gathered her. Miz Mac roped her and snubbed her to a post, got back on her horse, roped both hind feet, and stretched the critter out. With the saddle horse keeping the rope tight, she used a sharpened tablespoon as a knife to remove the diseased eye. Packing the space full of rock salt, she sewed the eyelid together and turned the cow out. In a week she was healed.

"I never saw this done again until 1960, by Dr. Skow, a vet from Raton. He had much more modern equipment, but didn't do any better job than Miz Mac did with her tablespoon. I told him about her surgery, and he said a vet probably would not have even attempted it at that time.

"That summer I had the opportunity of working for a very special person. I kept in touch with her from then on, until she passed away after living a full life in July of 1985. I was honored to be a pallbearer at her funeral and still think of her often.

"She understood people, horses and cattle as well as anyone I've ever known. She was firm if she needed to be but was always gentle, loving and caring. I'm only one of many people whose lives Miz Mac touched by her giving of knowledge and common sense, as well as her many accomplishments for her county, state and country. I know the things that I observed and the things that Miz Mac taught me have made me a better person and livestock man today."

15 Through the Eyes of Her Family

Miz Mac's family always came first with her — her grand-parents, parents, brothers and sisters; then her husband and her own children; then the grandchildren, and on down the line. She loved each of them, always putting their interests and welfare to the forefront.

Although she rarely spoke of hardships, frightening moments, or hard times, they were also a part of her life, and her family members recall them, along with the small, day-to-day happenings which speak so eloquently of Bernice McLaughlin.

Son Stanley shared some of his reminisces:

"When I was quite young, possibly 1 1/2 or 2 years old, I was play-ing in a hand-dug cellar at home. Suddenly, one wall of the cellar caved in. I was completely buried. My daddy and our family dog started dig-ging frantically. By the time they rescued me, I had already turned blue from lack of oxygen, so I really had a narrow escape!

"At the age of 2 1/2 or 3, I was playing outdoors with my dog, close to the North kitchen window. After a while I went into the house and asked Mother for a piece of bread. She gave it to me and I returned to play. The barking of our dog attracted Mother's attention, and she looked out the window to discover me laughing as I tore off pieces of the bread and dropped them down on a coiled rattlesnake.

"Dashing out the door and around the house, she grabbed me up and ran away from the snake. Her intense fear naturally frightened me, and I've been very much afraid of snakes every since.

"In the late '40's, Mother was wintering cattle about 11 miles from the ranch. She often rode down there on horseback to check on them and to feed. One such ride was made on a bright sunny day after a heavy snow, which had blanketed the entire country.

"She did not wear sun glasses, and after arriving home from her ride, she realized the unusual brightness had damaged her eyes, so she called me. I was living and working at Cimmaron Station, about 20 miles North of the ranch. The snow was very deep, so I borrowed the company winch truck to drive to the ranch.

"I picked her up and went back via Grenville and into Clayton, anxious to get her to the doctor. The roads were extremely bad, but we finally made it to town. The doctor treated Mother's eyes, and she recovered nicely.

"We later discovered that Patrolman Earl Morris of the New Mexico State Police and some of the state highway crew had also attempted to reach the ranch and get her to a doctor, but their efforts were in vain.

"They came out the Mountain road, breaking trail with a Caterpillar tractor, which towed the police car. By the time they reached the ranch, we had already left by the other route. They spent from 10:30 am to 9 pm getting from Clayton to the ranch and back, which gives you some idea of the winter road conditions Mother sometimes experienced.

"The weather often caused serious problems on the ranch. One Friday night during the extremely cold winter of 1956, Mother phoned to say it was 18 degrees below zero and all her water pipes in the house were frozen; even though some of them were under the house. I was living in Colorado at the time, and it was 125 miles to the ranch.

"I gathered up blow torch and other equipment to work with and drove down. We worked the rest of the night thawing out water lines. By the time I finished it was morning, and Mother had breakfast ready. After breakfast we checked the pastures, finding two wells frozen up. The jerk rods were broken, so the rest of the day was spent getting them back in working order. Mother was very grateful to get everything put back together."

Stanley's wife, Marjorie, remembered her mother-in-law as willing and generous.

"There was no job too small or too large for Mama Mac to tackle. Whatever the task, she was always willing to help. I've often seen her work for hours picking, sorting, and canning fruit and vegetables. After all that work, she was ever ready to share with friends, neighbors and relatives.

"Our second daughter arrived more than a month before she was expected. We were living at the McLaughlin ranch home, and Reba decided to make her appearance during one of those September downpours when all the creeks were running bank-full. This was 1937 and

Aunt Martha with Wanda, Stanley and friends.

there was no bridge across the Corrumpa Creek, so we could not reach either doctor or hospital.

"Stanley drove through the mud to a neighbor's home and brought Ruth Moore. Between her and Mama Mac and their mid-wife talents, Reba came into the world without any difficulties. Their care and concern were deeply appreciated in that time of need.

"Mama Mac enjoyed keeping our two daughters, which enabled Stanley and me to enjoy short trips, ball games and other activities together.

"Although she was basically fearless, I recall one incident in which she reacted like a normal woman. It was in the early '50's, and summertime. My sister Anna and her husband and two daughters were visiting us. We'd all driven over to the ranch for supper. A sudden downpour came, and it rained hard for a few hours.

"After dark, although she'd taken her shoes off to relax, Mama Mac decided to make the short trip outside to check the rain gauge and see how much it had rained. Just outside the West living room door, she screamed, scaring herself as well as the rest of us.

"Someone grabbed a flashlight and discovered that Mama Mac had stepped on a slimy old water dog [*salamander*]. One of the young neices, Peggy, was so frightened by Mama Mac's scream and fright that she began to cry loudly. We all had a good laugh when things calmed down.

"The old saying, 'A friend in need is a friend indeed' truly applied to this wonderful woman, loved by her family and friends."

Miz Mac's daughter Wanda shared the following recollections.

"When I was very young I remember Mother, Stanley and I riding old Badger or going places in the little buggy or wagon. We went to Sunday school at Prairie Dale school house, and Mother played the old pump organ.

"One very muddy day after a rain, as Mother and Badger took us to school at Circle Valley, we were going down a steep hill and Badger slipped. Stanley and I fell off, but Mother's foot went through the stirrup. She was wearing shoes with a button strap. Badger spooked and ran and she was dragged for about 100 yards, until the strap of her shoe broke. We were all scared and she was bruised up, but not hurt seriously.

"Mother always made our clothes. Once she worked most of the night to finish a pretty pink organdy dress for me to wear for a picnic down at the Wight place. I was very proud of my pretty dress, but during the picnic I got so involved playing games and climbing trees with the other kids that I didn't realize what was happening to my dress. Too late, I discovered I'd completely ruined it. I was really sad, and Mother was, too, but she didn't punish me because she realized I hadn't done it on purpose.

"A frightening incident was related to Mother's sewing. I was quite small, and was playing on the floor while she sewed. I reached under

The "favorite" teacher, Mattie Blake, ready to drive Wanda and Stanley to school.

the sewing machine treadle to retrieve a toy just as it came down, cutting my finger off. She looked out and saw a car coming, so ran up the road and stopped it. It was Mr. Kendrick, and he came down and held me while she put my finger back on. She poured turpentine on it and tied it up real tight, and I still have it. She could always keep a cool head and think and act quickly.

"A special treat I recall Mother making for us in the evenings or on winter days was brown sugar candy! She also made good lightbread and cinnamon buns, and sometimes there would be hot ones to eat when we got home from school. They tasted so good.

"Mother also made soap. She would save all the old grease and in the summertime we'd make a fire out in the yard and put the big black kettle on it. We'd cook the grease in there and put lye in it, and it really made good soap.

"When I was in first grade, Aunt Martha came to live with us. Our teacher, Mattie Blake also lived with us, and it was a special time when we all had a lot of fun. We drove the little buggy with one horse to school. Mattie taught at Circle Valley two years and was my favorite teacher. During that time we had a lot of fun programs at school. When she left we all cried as we sang, 'God be with you 'till we meet again.'

"I recall going to a Christmas program at the Guy school, about 12 miles away. It was real cold weather, and we wrapped heated rocks and stove lids and put them in the bottom of the wagon to help keep our feet warm.

"Until I was about 10-years-old we had a hired girl to keep house and do the cooking. Even so, Mother saw to it that I learned how, and I took over the job when I was ten. I made some messes, but Mother was always understanding, and would help me out of them.

"She also taught me to help in the field. I learned to run the knife sled, pull beans, and shock feed.

"Mother knew how to teach you a lesson you wouldn't forget. Once, she sent me to the post office for the mail, on foot, about a mile. Begley's ran the post office and also had a store. I saw some pretty blue and white glass beads there, and I wanted a string of them so bad. I asked Mrs. Begley if I could have them and pay her later, and she let me have them.

"I walked the mile home and proudly showed the pretty beads to Mother. She scolded me, saying 'We don't do business that way!', and set me hiking right back to the store, to return the beads. About a month later Mother got the beads for me, but I'd learned a business lesson I've never forgotten — to operate on the cash basis only.

Stanley and Marjorie McLaughlin and daughters, Reba and Beulah.

"Each fall, we went to the brakes for wood. This was about a ten mile trip, to an area near the dripping springs. It was beautiful country. We always took the team and wagon and packed a lunch because we'd stay all day getting wood to haul home for winter. We also liked to go there just for picnics when Mattie and Aunt Martha lived with us, and the Chilcotes also accompanied us sometimes.

"I always liked to ride horseback. We used to make our horses jump soapweeds, I guess because we'd heard Mother say it was fun to jump horses. We rode to school and Prairie Dale and Cuates. When Uncle Earl left he gave his horse Redwing and his saddle to Stanley, so then we each had a saddle.

"For many years we had only the saddle Mother brought from Canada, purchased with the money she earned riding race horses there. Riley restored that saddle a few years ago and we still have it. It is now displayed at the Museum in Clayton.

"When I was about 11-years-old we drove into Clayton and saw a big trimotor airplane out East. A barnstormer was giving rides for $5 each. We drove out to see the plane, and Stanley and I begged Mother to let us take a ride. We really couldn't afford it, but Mother always found a way. She finally said, 'Well, all right. But we'll all go. If that plane goes down we will all go.' So, we rode the airplane and it was a big thrill.

"Coming from the foothills of the beautiful Canadian Rockie's, Mother naturally loved trees. When I was small, we'd go down to the creek and dig up little cottonwood trees, take them home, and plant them. We had to carry water in buckets to help them grow – but we had trees! After the dustbowl days, the Soil Conservation Service gave Chinese Elm trees, so we planted more trees and watered them with buckets.

"Mother was always proud of the Triple Link brand Daddy had registered, similar to the emblem of the IOOF Lodge, which he was evidently very proud to belong to. Mother was always the one to put the brand on, because she wanted it to look good, and it was easy to blotch if it wasn't done just right. We still own the brand with the ranch.

"Branding day was always an occasion for a good time. All the family helped, and neighbors also came to help.

"We worked hard milking cows and raising pigs and saved enough money to buy a new Model A Ford car. Stanley and I started to high school at Seneca, which was a 20 mile drive one way. There were no school buses in our part of the country, so we drove the new car.

"Cars didn't have heaters then, and one morning Stanley's hands got too cold, so I was driving. I was just 13. There was a little snow on the ground, making it slick, and the road was real rough in places. I lost control and totally wrecked the car. Stanley drove it home and put it in the garage before Mother saw it. When she found out, she was naturally upset – but told us she was just thankful we weren't hurt.

"I thank the Lord every day for the inspiration Mother was to me and the wonderful heritage she left for her family."

Miz Mac's first granddaughter, Beulah McLaughlin Hittson, wrote the following, titled "My Fondest memories of Grandmother (Mama Mc)."

"We lived about 1 1/2 miles from her until I was 6 years old. I remember her riding in on horseback to visit us. She usually found time to take me for a ride. It might not be very far, but was always the highlight of my day.

"Then Daddy went to work for Colorado Interstate Gas Company at Clayton Station, and we moved into Clayton, 28 miles from her. We lived there for several years. Whenever Daddy had time off we went to the ranch to see Grandmother and help her in any way we could. She also came in to visit us when she could. We'd always beg her to spend the night with us, but she usually had chores to do at home. If it was on a weekend or summertime, I managed to go home with her whenever possible.

"When Daddy got a promotion with his job we moved to Cimarron Station which was 20 miles North of the ranch. We'd pass by there going to town so would get to see her about once a week. I spent all the time I could with her. It was always a treat to help her feed the cows and see the new-born calves.

"Early summer brought branding time, when I would get to ride horseback and help gather the cattle. The calves were flanked by hand, and I can remember sitting on the ground, holding the hind leg of the calf while Grandmother did the branding herself.

"I also recall going with her to milk the cows, and arguing with my sister Reba as to whose turn it was to turn the crank on the cream separator. Grandmother milked several cows and sold the cream for a living. She also taught me how to milk at an early age. I had my husband convinced that I didn't know how to milk, until it was mentioned in front of Grandmother and he found out differently!

"She always took time out to entertain us. She often took us to the West pasture where there was a nice stream of living water so we could wade. Returning, we'd usually stop and visit the neighbors, Lawson and Viola Long.

"Several times Grandmother and I plowed muddy roads all the way from Clayton, only to get to the Corrumpa Creek and find it running bank to bank. We'd have to sit in the car several hours, waiting for it to run down enough so we could cross it. There were usually some good snacks among her groceries, but there might not be any left by the time we got home.

"Later, Grandmother was the one who got the Highway Department to put a bridge across the creek and it was named after her.

"She would ride into Clayton, bringing several other saddle horses with her, so she and her family could be in the July 4 parade. She had no way to haul the horses, but that didn't stop her.

"I spent a lot of time with her in the summer, and always seemed to get nominated to cook the dinner. She would usually tell me what to cook and how to do it, then go to the field to plow or whatever else she might be doing. I give her a lot of credit in my learning how to cook, clean house, and garden. During spring cleaning, I always got the job of cleaning out the kitchen cupboards.

"In 1953 I married Billy Hittson and moved to Des Moines, where we still live, about 30 miles West of Grandmother's. We continued to help her anytime we could with cattle work, etc. She was always here when we needed, her, too.

"We remodeled a house we had moved to the ranch and she made many a trip up to help us work on it. Her neighbor, Mr. Kendrick, did carpenter work. She'd bring him up and they would both work hard all day.

"When we first married, Grandmother gave us a buckskin mare, 'Dot', and wanted us to raise a colt. She had a real good sorrel horse colt which we named 'Brandy.' He turned out to be a nice, gentle horse that helped raise our children.

"Grandmother always looked forward to family gatherings at her house for Thanksgiving or Christmas. I presented her with three great-grandchildren and before she passed on she enjoyed three of my grand-children, her great-great-grand's. We had five-generation pictures taken.

"There was never a job too big for Grandmother to tackle. she was always there to help anyone that needed help. She loved her ranch, her lovely home and all her family. We all loved her dearly, and a day never goes by that I don't think of her."

Miz Mac's other granddaughter, Reba Mc Laughlin Garrison, wrote the following "Recollections of Grandmother."

"Grandmother started me out young riding horses. She would ride horseback up to where we lived at the old Donner place, about 1 1/2 miles from her ranch. I was probably about 3-years-old when she let me ride her horse back to the ranch by myself. The horse was a grey gelding named Badger.

Old Badger, about 1942, babysitting Beulah, Reba, and Loris, his third generation of McLaughlins.

"My love of horses started with Badger, as he would put his head down for me to bridle him, and always stood still while I climbed on a fence to get on him. I don't really remember how old I was when Grandmother traded Badger for a hot water heater. What a loss!

"Speaking of badgers, Grandmother caught a baby badger one spring while she was out feeding cattle. He was quite a pet. He played with the dogs and scared a lot of people, especially the women who came to Grandmother's for 'club' meetings. She had him all one summer, until he started visiting the chicken house at night. Needless to say, Grandmother wouldn't put up with that. 'Shorty' sure was cute while he lasted.

"When I was about 10-years-old, Grandmother gave me a baby colt. She asked what I wanted to name him and I told her 'Trigger.' She liked the name 'Pecos' better, so that was what he was called. He was a blood bay with black points.

"When Pecos was about 3-years-old, he was injured by kicking over the top of a barbed wire fence. He cut one hind leg right in the joint. Grandmother decided she could doctor him and he would recover. Other people thought he should be shot. She doctored him for two years. He dragged the leg for a year, but finally started using it.

"When Pecos was a 5-year-old, Grandmothers nephew Loris Walsh came down from Canada for a visit, and he started breaking Pecos. He was a handful, and not very trustworthy. The summer after Loris went back to Canada, I started riding Pecos. He had so much stamina you needed to ride him hard every day.

"My family had moved to Cimarron Station by this time, so Grandmother let me take Pecos up there. She put me on him early one morning and said not to stop or get off of him until I got to the first cattleguard, which was about 12 miles up the road. By the time I got there he had calmed down enough to where I could get back on him after closing the gate.

"Another eight miles and three cattleguards later, I made it home. Pecos was ridden every day that summer and still was not foolproof. He could translate sideways and you never knew what scared him.

"I put up some barrels in a lot close to the barn, and started training him for barrel racing. He took to it immediately, and loved running.

"The next summer, Grandmother started taking me to local rodeos. Pecos did very well in barrel racing and Grandmother was my cheering squad. She never missed a rodeo I rode in. We went to Des Moines, Grenville, Clayton, Hayden, Dalhart, Trinidad, Cimarron, etc. with Pecos riding in the bed of the pickup. We had to put the saddle on him and tie him to the pickup rack as he liked to sway from side to side.

Granddaughter Reba McLaughlin running barrels on Pecos.

The second summer of rodeoing Grandmother bought a trailer, so loading and unloading were much simpler.

"The first year of rodeoing I rode Pecos into Clayton before the rodeo there. Grandmother said he needed the exercise to calm him down. It took me six hours to get to town from the ranch.

"In the fall of 1953 I was the Union County candidate for State Fair Queen. Pecos went to the big city of Albuquerque! He was embarassingly spooky and held up part of the State Fair Parade by refusing to go through the railroad underpass. I eventually got him through, and made it back to the State Fair Grounds. I didn't win, but sure had a lot of fun.

"I rodeoed for three summers, 1953 through 1955. When I was making marriage plans in the fall of 1955 I advertised Pecos for sale at the Trinidad Rodeo. He was purchased there by Dora Waldrop of Amarillo, TX. After my marriage we moved to Amarillo and, thanks to Dora's generosity, I was able to ride Pecos that year. Dora continued to rodeo on him until he was about 20-years-old.

"Grandmother always had a love for all animals, but especially a good horse. She was never without a horse around the place, and still had one when she died."

Wanda's son, Bill, had the following recollections about his grandmother. "Numerous events come to mind when remembering my Grandmother and days spent out at the ranch. Winters were cold. Chores early in the morning were especially dreadful on a boy 8 or 10. A trip to hunt coyotes or rabbits, however, with anyone who could drive, and was willing, were met with wide eyes and exhilaration. Summers were hard work, work and hard play. Work meant pulling endless weeds and blisters big as quarters. Play meant cool streams to wade in and sour cherries off the tree. There were always minnows to catch, lizards to chase, and birds to shoot with a BB gun. There was the occasional tinkle of a window pane caused by the missed direction of a BB; usually taken in stride by Gama. Well, half stride anyway.

"One account of innocent mischief was brought to the attention of my Grandmother, although quite unknowingly by myself at the time. It was just before lunch time and my approach to soften the words that came with hands thrown in the air was to convince everyone how hungry I was for fried chicken, and what a fine treat it would be for everyone. I was trying to hurry this discussion along as much as possible because by now the chicken my dog had run laps on until it dropped, was on the verge of going stiff. After quickly seeing through my nerves of spaghetti and hiding eyes, I was told to follow and was led straight to the scene of the crime. How did she know? The walk to the chicken house took about three days and after taking my verbal abuse with hands behind my back and eyes boring deep holes in the ground I looked up to see Gama smiling and asking, 'How do you like your chicken? Fried I guess!' "

Loris Hughes, Wanda's elder son, had many thoughts to share about his grandmother.

"I called her 'Gama.' That name stuck because our relationship didn't change. She never became a different person to me as I grew older, which seemed unusual. She must've always treated me as a equal, not as a child. We had a very special relationship.

"Gama was always caring for animals and human beings. I had a cow at her ranch, a heifer which was given to me by my Grandad Hughes, and Gama kept it for me. She had a calf every year, and when I was five or six I was visiting Gama and we had a tremendous hailstorm. My calf evidently got bonked on the head by a very large hailstone and we found it wandering alone in a field, very addled.

"Gama immediately brought it to the barn and we doctored it. It must've had some kind of concussion. I sat up with it two or three days running, but the fifth or sixth day it completely recovered.

"Wayne Lawrence (whom we called 'Sonny'), Howard Hughes, and myself had a 'cousin's reunion' at Gama's ranch a couple of weeks each summer for several years. We had all sorts of experiences, and I'm sure some of our wild ideas for entertainment came from Gama as she strove to keep three boys busy.

"Four or five old wagons had accumulated around the ranch, hand-me-downs from who-knows-where. We appropriated these as our 'chariots,' and would push them off the hill and 'race' them to the bottom. Ben Hur would've been proud of us, I'm sure! First of all, we'd spend several days getting the chariots into peak racing condition, oiling the hubs, and making sure they'd run perfectly. Riding the wagons down the hill as fast as we could go often resulted in a spill at the bottom.

"Even that was boring after a while, so we decided to hook our chariots up to Gama's milk pen calves. We'd get ropes on them and tie them to our wagons, and round and round we'd go. It seemed like we were racing—probably we weren't going very fast at all.

"I vividly recall coming around a curve and meeting the snubbing post head on, crashing my chairot—all to the glee of my watching grandmother.

"Wagons occupied a large portion of our time. Sonny and I devised an even more daredevil pastime, riding the wagons off the roof of the barn. We'd bring them up to the high pitch, help each other get on board and down we would go. We only tried that once or twice because Sonny wound up with a very large bump on his head that had to be doctored by Gama.

"My grandmother enjoyed a rodeo or somebody getting on a bronc, a bucking calf, bull or milk cow more than most anyone. After my Freshman year at college I brought a friend, Jerry Kimzey home to spend the summer. He was gon'na teach me how to ride broncs and bulls. Of course we were at Gama's ranch, and several times a week we'd get five or six cows into the corral, herd them into the working chute, and tie a rope around them. All of this was with Gama's approval; in fact she was usually the one to open the gate and cheer us on.

"She certainly wouldn't let us use spurs but some of those old cows got pretty good. I don't think the cowboys improved much or learned much about bullriding, but we certainly had a lot of fun and provided a lot of entertainment for Gama. Looking back, I'm amazed that she allowed us to ride her registered Hereford cattle, running the risk of injuring or killing one. To her, it was just too much fun to miss out on.

"I have fond memories of Mr. Kendrick, too, in fact he became my surrogate grandad. He was the grandfather of my cousin Howard Hughes, and he and his wife lived 5 miles North of my grandmother. Some years after he was widowed, he became Gama's hired hand. I remember him being around the ranch from the time I was 8 or 9-years-old until well after I graduated from high school.

"One very vivid memory is of coming in from the hayfield with a big wagonload of hay being pulled behind the pickup. Mr. Kendrick decided he should ride up there to make sure the load didn't shift. About halfway home it sure enough shifted. In fact, the entire pile of hay slid right off the wagon. Mr. Kendrick rode it all the way down, right into the middle of the road. It set him down as easy as if he'd been on a feather bed.

"My grandmother really enjoyed telling stories, and I've heard this one so many times I'm not sure if I was there or only heard about it. It is as vivid in my mind as if I had been there, but I doubt if I was. I was the happy recipient of many stories about many people from Gama.

"Gama had a wonderful philosophy of life. She told me always to try again. As I watched her live life I saw consistency in that approach. She would accept failure readily and move up out of the failure to try the same thing over again.

"There are many examples of that, but perhaps most vividly illustrative to me were her efforts to get a road paved from Clayton to the Colorado line. She worked on that probably 30 years out of her life, meeting with New Mexico highway officials, soliciting support from people who lived along the road, meeting with county officials in Union County and highway officials in Colorado. Of course a paved road from Clayton to the ranch would have been a small benefit to her personally, but she worked well beyond that.

She always had a project—something that was taking and occupying her time. If she failed, she got up and tried again. I saw this lived

From left, Wanda, Bill, Riley and Loris Hughes.

out over and over, and it had a solid impact on my life. I consider it a major plus, from Gama to me.

"She lived out 'try anything.' I think it was born of necessity. She was widowed at a young age with kids to raise, farming to do, and the responsibilities of running a ranch, including the care of chickens, pigs, milk cows, beef cattle, building fence, fixing automobiles, repairing the house, plumbing, etc. She was not aftaid to try to fix or to do any particular thing and many times she was able in her own unique way to accomplish it. Most of the time she did a quality job of whatever she attempted.

"Gama wasn't afraid to ask people to help her, either. She was willing to do what it took to make sure her and hers got along, and that included us grandchildren. She wanted her family to have the things they needed. Mabye not everything they wanted, but what they needed, even if it meant asking people to help. She spent a lot of time working with all of us and teaching us to do many different kinds of things.

"From 7 to 12 years of age I spent much of my time at the ranch running around under the trees shooting at birds with my Daisy beebee gun. Gama seemed to know how much enjoyment I got from this, so she encouraged me in it. Once, as luck would have it, I shot a sparrow and it fell from the tree. Now, I'd seen people hunt quail and ducks, so in my own boy way I decided I should clean my kill. I proudly brought it to the house to show Gama and she was elated—to the point that she thought we should have it for lunch. She cooked it up like she would have cooked a chicken, and she even helped me eat it for lunch.

"When I think about images of my grandmother, I see a lady of iron, all five foot four inches of her. She was hard on projects, and easy on people (for the most part). She had an iron willed determination. If she set something in motion she did her very best to see it through to completion. She had an iron fist. If she got a grip on something she never let it go. She wore iron boots. She was fearless to walk into any kind of situation. If she felt it was the right thing to do, she'd be there.

"That image speaks to me strongly of her persistent nature. She was exceptionally persistent. She wanted to help me learn the piano. I vividly recall her reminders. She asked not one question or offered not one reminder but two or three times a week she asked how I was coming with my piano. Sometimes, like every kid, I sure didn't wish to practice, but because of her persistent reminders I practiced a lot more than I would have otherwise.

"Finally, I remember the spiritual side of Gama. She was always very open about sharing life's experiences, and would talk with us about a variety of matters.

"She and I were baptized in the same water. [*Miz Mac had made a public profession of her faith when her own children were small, at the little country schoolhouse which served as their worship center, but of course there was no baptistry there!*] I was 13 and Gama was 62. I clearly remember that Sunday evening in August at the 1st Baptist Church in Clayton. Gama and I were the only ones in the baptistry. In fact, we were in the water at the same time and the minister, E.J. Kearney, made a very special memory of it, and a special moment for both of us.

"She really didn't preach to anyone. The only expression of Jesus Christ alive and active in her life was the way she lived it. Her faith spoke most loudly to me and to many people around her in the consistent way she visited the sick. About every Sunday afternoon after church, she'd go visit the Old Folks Home or those who were sick and in the hospital.

"She'd use the term 'old folks', and it often meant people 20 to 25 years younger than her 75 or 80 years. That was a mindset she had. She was not old because old is just a state of mind, and she never envisioned herself that way.

"Her spirituality really was expressed in the way she lived her life. Take the 'Good Samaritan' aspect. Always, she was helping someone. As a young person I was often amazed at how many people were always at the ranch, for meals or maybe just living there, often for two or three weeks or a month. If somebody came by and needed something she had, she'd give it away. If any came by and were without, she provided for their needs from what she had.

"Watching her interact with the people who passed by her ranchhouse on the road, I saw the teachings of Jesus in action. If they were sick, hungry, needed a cool drink, or just a word of encouragement, she provided. If they needed a place to stay for a week or a month she provided, and in some cases for a year or two. Her home and her heart were always open to helping other people.

"That is the legacy of my wonderful Gama."

Five generations. From left, Miz Mac, Stanley McLaughlin, Beulah Hittson, and daughter Barbara and her son Travis.

16   Trail's End

F rom November 27, 1891, to July 10, 1985, Bernice Walsh McLaughlin broke a lot of prairie trails for those who came behind; trails which spanned two nations, both of which she called home.

Prairie trailbreaking in her era took strength, a special kind of strength. A strength which was itself born of adversity and trial, and which bred toughness, tenacity, determination and courage.

In an August, 1971 article by Dorothy Sullins, New Mexico Farm and Ranch magazine saluted the pioneers of Union County, New Mexico, Miz Mac's home for the greater part of her lifetime. We quote from that article:

" 'Adversity,' according to an old saying, 'builds character.' This is probably nowhere truer than in the southwestern United States and in Union County, New Mexico.

" 'Drought,' 'Dustbowl,' and 'Depression' are the three character-building 'D's' of the grasslands. In Union County whenever people talk about the past, or the future, the three 'D's' pop into the conversation. The youth of Union County are the inheritors of what those who persisted and survived the three 'D's' will leave."

Miz Mac was lauded in that magazine article, as one of those who "persisted and survived." She told them, "I was in debt to the bank most of my life, but I'm finally out!"

Miz Mac survived the 'three D's' partly because she'd already found her own deep wells of inner strength. She had been forced to learn how to survive, in the face of earlier and harder tests.

She survived partly because she understood and always practiced God's laws of reaping and sowing. She faithfully sowed love – and reaped it in abundance, from her family and a host of friends.

She faithfully sowed generosity, and helpfulness—and reaped the same in abundance. She understood and obeyed "Give, and it shall be given unto you, full measure, pressed down, running over," and "With whatsoever measure you mete, it will be meted unto you." What little she had, she was willing to share or to give outright to anyone who needed it. She was a cheerful giver.

Miz Mac understood the wisdom of Solomon's Proverbs which say "two are better than one" and "a cord of three strands is not easily broken." She eagerly reached out to help those around her, and was not too proud to accept, or even to ask for, help in return.

She faithfully carried out Jesus' admonishment to "do it unto the least of these" by feeding the hungry, giving drink to the thirsty, clothing the needy, and visiting the sick and shut in.

Miz Mac had strong convictions, and she stood for them. If she had a problem with you, she'd confront you about it, rather than telling everyone else.

She never "sounded a trumpet before her," but performed her neighborly deeds and gave her generous gifts quietly, and without fanfare. She would've been embarrased by that.

Ever active, and interested in her world to her last breath, Miz Mac infused others with her contagious enthusiasm for living. Her legacy is rich indeed.

"Hard work never hurt anybody."

"Always keep trying."

"Believe in God and in yourself and you can do anything."

"All things are possible."

Dorothy Sullins concluded her New Mexico Farm and Ranch article by saying, "Union County, like steel, has been tested and found strong. Those who have survived are the ones who have been able to adapt, innovate, cooperate, and persist."

Miz Mac was one of those.

J. F. Clarke has written, "Progress, in the sense of acquisition, is something; but progress in the sense of being is a great deal more. To grow higher, deeper, wider, as the years go on; to conquer difficulties and acquire more and more power; to feel all one's faculties unfolding and truth descending into the soul—this makes life worth living."

Miz Mac's prairie trails are well-marked by progress. The comfortable, successful Triple Link Ranch testifies to that progress in the sense of acquisition. The honors she won and a large, successful and well-respected family and an innumerable host of friends testify to her progress in the sense of being.

Bernice Walsh McLaughlin's life truly was "worth living." The lives of all who follow in her prairie trails have been, and will continue to be, enriched by the legacy she left.

All of Miz Mac's prairie trails led to her prairie home, the Triple Link Ranch. This is the final product, after expansion and landscaping.

Miz Mac was never happier than when she was with horses.

Order Form

NEED EXTRA COPIES OF *PRAIRIE TRAILS*?

Orders may be sent to:

Quarter Circle A Enterprises
1159 State Highway 450
Newcastle, WY 82701

or

Wanda Hughes
105 Court Street
Clayton, NM 88415

Sales tax:
Please add state sales tax for books to be shipped to New Mexico or Wyoming addresses (4% in Wyoming).

Shipping:
Book Rate: $1.50 for the first book and $1.00 for each additional book. Air Mail: $2.25 per book.

Payment:
Please enclose your check or money order.

Name _____

Address _____

City _____ State _____ Zip _____